REBUILDING THE FOUNDATIONS

REBUILDING THE FOUNDATIONS

*Social Relationships
in Ancient Scripture and
Contemporary Culture*

JOHN BRUEGGEMANN
AND
WALTER BRUEGGEMANN

WESTMINSTER
JOHN KNOX PRESS
LOUISVILLE · KENTUCKY

First edition
Published by Westminster John Knox Press
Louisville, Kentucky

17 18 19 20 21 22 23 24 25 26—10 9 8 7 6 5 4 3 2 1

Book design by Erika Lundbom-Krift
Cover design by Mark Abrams

Library of Congress Cataloging-in-Publication Data

Names: Brueggemann, John, 1965-, author. | Brueggemann, Walter, 1965- author.
Title: Rebuilding the foundations : social relationships in ancient scripture and contemporary culture / John Brueggemann and Walter Brueggemann.
Description: First edition. | Louisville, Kentucky : Westminster John Knox Press, [2017]
Identifiers: LCCN 2016041540 (print) | LCCN 2016048632 (ebook) | ISBN 9780664262655 (pbk. : alk. paper) | ISBN 9781611647884 (ebk.)
Subjects: LCSH: Sociology, Biblical. | United States—Social conditions—21st century. | United States—Economic conditions—21st century. | United States—Moral conditions—21st century
Classification: LCC BS670 .B78 2017 (print) | LCC BS670 (ebook) | DDC 261.0973—dc23
LC record available at https://lccn.loc.gov/2016041540

Most Westminster John Knox Press books are available at special quantity discounts when purchased in bulk by corporations, organizations, and special-interest groups. For more information, please e-mail SpecialSales@wjkbooks.com.

for
James Bonner Brueggemann
our well-beloved son and brother

CONTENTS

ACKNOWLEDGMENTS

As with all my professional endeavors, this work benefited from the support of my colleagues in the Department of Sociology at Skidmore College. I want to gratefully acknowledge helpful feedback on this project from Andrew Lindner and Pat Oles. I also want to thank Shannon Reilly for painstaking research assistance and incisive editing.

I have had many gifted and generous teachers, including my older brother, Jim. There was no time when he was not there. I can remember learning countless things from him—how to share, throw a baseball, basketball, or football, write letters, use a credit card, and be a good host, for example. Some of the lessons were painful, like learning the price of borrowing a valued shirt without asking. And lots of them were fun, like how to skip a rock in a pond, buy concert tickets, or make a proper margarita.

Now that I have my own kids, I know that I was learning from him all the time, throughout our childhood, often without realizing it. Much of what I know about decency, integrity, friendship, and leadership was initially modeled by my bother. I am immensely grateful for the ongoing lessons, laughter, and sharing of life. This book is dedicated to him.

Another great teacher in my life, needless to say, is my coauthor. To this day, I learn something every time I am with my father. As I look back, the only time I was not learning from him (or was not aware of learning from him) was during my teenage years. Throughout that period, as Jim can attest, Dad became amazingly stupid, while I knew everything (Jim may not agree with that part). Later, he somehow became really smart again and I knew less.

Among the many insights Dad relayed to me was an awareness of the Bible, the communities it nurtured, and the God at the center of their lives. These sensibilities were in the air as long as I can remember. But they were also somehow challenging, durable, and thick at the same time.

This was clarified for me a couple years back when I read a message written by a former student and friend of my father's.

> In his teaching, preaching, and writing, Walter testifies to a deep and abiding relationship with the biblical text, and with the vexing, awesome, awful God who cannot be disentangled from the text, who seems to grasp him without ever quite being grasped. He puts

on the Bible like an old coat—not a comfortable barn jacket, let alone a glorious garment of many colors, but a well-worn, coarse and woolly thrift store coat that never quite fits. It pinches, scratches, bunches, and binds. It's a little too warm in the summer and not warm enough in the winter. And it's never really in style. Yet there's no imagining him going out without it.

This characterization sounded right to me. And I know Dad loved it. It is not just about his engagement with the Word, but also captures something about Dad's eccentric, scholarly, or, at times, monastic proclivities. (This is a guy who spends a lot of time in the basement by himself!) It occurred to me that the "old coat" has a bunch of sociological threads. It is a splendid gift to be able to collaborate on this project with him.

John Brueggemann

THIS FATHER, LIKE EVERY FATHER, TAKES GREAT DELIGHT IN being able to work at a project with his son. The interface between John and me is a lively one. On the one hand, I have long been interested in sociological work and continue to read in the field. Sociology was my undergraduate major (with my ancient esteemed teacher, Th. W. Mueller, to whom I remain greatly indebted), and I pondered for a time graduate study in the field. I did not pursue that study, but I am glad that John has. His work and his judgments have gone well beyond my learning or capacity in the discipline. On the other hand, from early on John has developed an acute theological sensibility, I think almost by osmosis in the church culture in which he was nurtured. Thus much of what I have labored hard to understand about theological claims he sees and grasps quite readily. Hence both John and I have investments in both of our disciplines. He has taken the lead in shaping this shared project. I am grateful to him . . . and proud of him as well!

I am glad that we can dedicate this book to Jim, our son and brother. While John and I have toiled over our books, Jim has chosen another way of living out his manhood, a way that tosses him about in the rough-and-tumble of the market. He has shown himself to be an agile participant in the life he has chosen, maintaining a tensive balance between the reality of the economy and the rootage of faith that he prizes. He practices that balance with uncommon grace and wisdom.

What better for this father than to have two such sons, one with whom to share a writing project, the other to be alive in knowing ways to the world as gift and as task. I am glad for an abiding connectedness to both of them, who I respect and cherish.

Walter Brueggemann

INTRODUCTION

<small>SOMETHING IS TORN IN THE FABRIC OF AMERICAN SOCIETY.</small> We lead the industrialized world in child poverty, food insecurity, homicide, incarceration, carbon dioxide emissions per capita, and the number of billionaires. Confidence in core institutions like government, business, unions, journalism, education, and the criminal justice system has reached record lows. Our leaders cannot seem to make decisions or pass laws that most citizens want. Ordinary people make choices destructive to themselves and one another. Gross domestic product goes up, but so many feel like they have less. The collusion of government and big quiet money has designed a redistribution system that leads to even greater concentrations of wealth, in turn resulting in the evaporation of the common good and the unbearable displacement

of vulnerable persons in the political economy. That extraction system now has global reach, so the displacements are global in scope.

How did we get to this point? What is it that really matters in our shared life? Why is it so hard to keep our attention on such things? What kinds of conversations must we have to reorient our lives? These are the concerns that animate this book. More specifically, what do sociology and biblical interpretation have to say about such matters? What do sociologists and biblical scholars have to say to one another? What common ground do they have? And where do they necessarily part ways?

In pursuing these matters, we have several goals in mind, listed here in no particular order. The first is autobiographical and confessional. As much as the essays below decry the moral disorder of our time, we seek to lay out our own struggles. Our interrogation is directed as much to our own assumptions and complacency as it is to anyone else's. We ourselves are habituated in a strong moral tradition; that moral tradition, however, is anemic in its present form in the face of these complexities that pose immense challenges. The problems of our time are not simply the result of some elemental evil force, but rather reflect a complicated historical moment in which the structural arrangements and cultural circumstances have been aligned to disastrous effects.

How we respond to this moment, individually and collectively, is a vexing challenge indeed. We proceed in the conviction that reframing these complex issues in a moral narrative that is critically informed and that does not evade the depth and complexity of the issues is work that is worth doing.

This is not an abstract set of social variables that intrigues us, but a lived experience with daily dilemmas. Do I have the right job? Am I working too hard? Saving enough? Are the pressures my boss or coworkers put on me legitimate? Am I asking the right things of my children? Am I pushing them too hard? What food should we be eating? What media should we be consuming? Am I volunteering enough? Donating enough? Is my household environmentally responsible? Am I compromising too much? Not enough? Am I advocating enough? Am I thinking clearly and imaginatively enough?

Together, such endless questions about how to live reflect something about modernity. Charles Derber calls it "the overburdened self." Michael Pollan talks about "the omnivore's dilemma," which relates to Barry Schwartz's broader notion of "the paradox of choice." Problems of scarcity and abundance are tied up in complicated ways. No, this is not merely about the collusion of a few greedy strongmen—though such efforts are certainly part of the problem. It is more complicated and involves all of us.

As personal as this topic is, we also have a modest theoretical agenda in this project. The framework for our commentary is derived from Jonathan Haidt's moral foundation theory. Haidt is a moral psychologist who has studied a broad range of evidence and arguments from archaeology, anthropology, biology, history, psychology, and sociology. He has also carried out a number of laboratory experiments testing and retesting the arguments that comprise this theory.

Based on this work, Haidt and his colleagues have identified six moral foundations (Haidt 2006, 2007, 2012; Haidt and Graham 2009; Haidt and Joseph 2004):

Care versus Harm
Fairness versus Cheating
Liberty versus Oppression
Loyalty versus Betrayal
Authority versus Subversion
Sanctity versus Degradation

All societies that endure must confront fundamental questions about how they are going to arrange themselves. Each foundational category represents a dilemma that must be negotiated to the satisfaction of most people. If sufficient members of a group believe that cheating, harm, oppression, betrayal, subversion, and/or degradation are too common, through the actions of either leaders or other individuals, turmoil is not far off.

This project is *not* intended to test, assess, or extend Haidt's theory. We hope that it will be useful in fleshing out the meaning of the concepts embedded in the theory by adding evidence and insights from academic disciplines other than psychology. Being deeply grounded as we are in a covenantal narrative that yields a moral theory, we find Haidt's exposition illuminating of our own moral grounding. Haidt has given specificity to the impulses that are very deep for us. Ultimately, though, we are borrowing moral foundation theory for our own use. The extent to which we do make a theoretical contribution will be a collateral benefit.

A related and more important goal is to illuminate

the moral disorder of our time. This is the most fundamental point of the project. We seek to bear witness to the unsustainable patterns of life in twenty-first-century America and suggest possibilities for reorientation. Such a reorientation does not depend on more technology or more advances in scientific awareness. At bottom we are humanists, albeit "believing" humanists. For that reason we believe that any significant shift will be reorientation that takes the neighbor seriously (including our nonhuman neighbors), that intends the flourishing of the neighborhood as common good, and that, in our tradition, is grounded in a vision of holy intention that undergirds, anticipates, and summons to neighborliness.

A secondary aim here is dialogical. Some might regard this exchange as strange: sociologists are all naive leftists; people who love the Bible are premodern rubes. Right? How could they talk to, let alone learn from, one another? But it could not be more natural for us. Walter, who is a biblical scholar, was a sociology major in college. John, who is a sociologist, grew up in a family of clergy (including a biblical scholar!). As father and son, we have both been breathing in these topics and talking about them for a long time. To sit down and think through such conversations and convert them into more systematically developed formulations has felt logical and energizing.

But the dialogical agenda here is more ambitious than our own conversation. As noted above, we ourselves grapple with the troubles laid out here. So many people, including the two of us, often find false comfort and confidence within a little subcultural bubble where our certitudes are reinforced by the like-minded. The imperative to engage in a discourse beyond such boundaries is central to this work.

Such dialogical discourse that may matter must cut below our usual mantras that we too readily reiterate. And when we go "below," what we find is the reality of human suffering and pain. Some of that human pain seems to be an inescapable given. Much of it is structurally and historically generated among us. In any case, we share the conviction that truth that may inform our social practice has a peculiar alliance with pain. And when truth is offered that is not filtered through the reality of pain, it must at least be suspect. The moral narrative in which we are situated has known about that alliance of truth and pain long before Foucault, but the critical theory that swirls around Foucault and his cohorts is much in the background of our probes.

We trust that a few sociologists who take the Bible seriously will feel like we are preaching to the choir. We have no doubt, moreover, that a company of Scripture interpreters with an acute interest in sociological analysis will join us in the same choir loft. But all choirs need rehearsal as well as encouragement, and, we suspect, ours is rather small. More broadly, we hope anyone interested in sociology, the Bible, or the state of society will find some resonance and perhaps insight here. Or at least a topic to debate.

What follows are six chapters based on the six moral foundations mentioned above. In a conclusion we reflect on the themes that emerge over the six chapters, explaining how sociology and biblical interpretation inform and intersect with one another and where they necessarily part ways.

Chapter 1

CARE

JB:* HAVE YOU EVER GONE FOR ANY EXTENDED TIME without water? Food? When you do, it is hard to think about anything else. Certainly not homework, electoral campaigns, win-loss records, or updating your status. Not even love. Taking care of our bodies is the most fundamental necessity in human society on which most everything else depends. The problem of care revolves around securing this basic building block for moral order.

The key here is that a critical mass of individuals have their material needs sufficiently met. The primary basis of this goal is elemental. Without physical sustenance, a person cannot function, and nothing else matters much.

*Sections designated JB were written by John Brueggemann. Sections designated WB were written by Walter Brueggemann. All else was coauthored.

7

If enough people are not adequately cared for, all of the contributions they would make for the group go unmet. In our context, think about what would happen without the work of farmers, doctors, teachers, police, clergy, or firefighters. What happens when parents do not parent?

At the most fundamental level, material security is an objective experience. You have enough calories to eat to live another day. But at some point after basic needs are met, the perception of such security becomes a subjective matter. We calibrate our needs in relation to the comparisons we associate with other people. If a person feels relatively deprived, disappointment follows. And sustained disappointment leads to disengagement. If enough people feel they are not getting what they need, the cohesion of society collapses. Relative poverty (or inequality) hurts the poor, of course, but it also costs the affluent by weakening institutions (e.g., distrust in politics) or burdening institutions (e.g., health care, criminal justice) (Wilkinson and Pickett 2009). In other words, psychological well-being requires a certain confidence that the group to which one belongs is concerned with the security of that individual. In *The Social System*, Talcott Parsons describes this issue in terms of the "biological prerequisites of individual life, like nutrition and physical safety. . . . These minimum needs of individual actors constitute a set of conditions to which the social system must be adapted" (1951, 28). The absence of such conditions is not functional.

There is a pattern in contemporary American society whose roots are so ancient, even prehistorical, that some people think it is an unchanging aspect of the human condition. It is the impulse to hoard resources. There is no culture without an economy. And every society has some kind of stratification system in which economic resources and opportunities are unevenly distributed to members of that society. Some are able to accumulate more assets than others.

The inequality resulting from class structure appears to many to reflect some kind of "natural" order. This perspective certainly has some merit. Individual ability and effort obviously contribute to one's life chances. Between two people in identical social circumstances, the more able one is more likely to thrive. On average, smarter, hardworking people accrue more economic resources than others. But such individual characteristics are themselves complicated. We have to consider intelligence, physical strength, work ethic, ruthlessness, honesty, and other innate and learned individual capacities. Plus there are various other factors in addition to personal qualities, which is to say, social circumstances are rarely identical across society. The different circumstances magnify the impact of various individual traits. Physical strength mattered more in Sparta than it does in Silicon Valley. A capacity for speaking different languages is more advantageous in India than it is in Indiana.

More generally, we see across cities, regions, and countries enormous disparities in the distribution of resources not based on individual ability. In other words, the capacity of individuals across such boundaries is not as varied as the inequality. Just because Finland has fewer citizens living in extreme poverty or extreme affluence compared to Brazil does not mean that there are proportionally many fewer really dumb or really smart Finns.

To consider the inequality immediately visible before us today as somehow normal and inevitable is to yield to a parochial, ahistorical sense of the world. Every society in the history of humanity has inequality, yes. But there are vast differences between the most egalitarian and the least egalitarian. Natural resources, technological development, education and credentialing processes, governance, taxation, social welfare, health care, internal and external security concerns, kinship networks, civic organizations, and cultural norms all represent social variables that affect how a stratification system will work.

Ancestral Maoris in New Zealand had a much more egalitarian economic system than that of contemporary, industrialized New Zealand, though their average material quality of life was lower due to less technological development. In the apartheid era of South Africa, or in Saudi Arabia today, a single characteristic greatly curtails a person's opportunities (race in the former case and gender in the latter). So there is always inequality. But it varies in important ways.

The United States has the highest rates of poverty—both in absolute and relative numbers—in the industrialized world. We have more income inequality and do less about it by way of government taxation and transfers compared to other industrialized countries (Gould and Wething 2012; Brown 2012).

The superrich control the vast majority of wealth. A recent Oxfam International report (Hardoon 2015) indicates that the richest 1 percent of people in the world own nearly half of all the wealth. In the United States, the top 1 percent owns 42 percent of all wealth. The true elite within that group, the top 0.1 percent, owns 22 percent (Saez and Zucman 2014).

A lot of those people are creative, hardworking, and determined. In some sense, they deserve big rewards. But a lot of them are not in the former group and do not deserve such rewards. We know that somewhere in the neighborhood of half of the richest Americans have inherited significant amounts of money (see Collins and Yeskel 2005; Moriarty et al. 2012). In *Capital in the Twenty-First Century*, Thomas Piketty argues that the normal pattern in free market capitalism is for the gains from inherited wealth to outpace the gains from earned wealth. That is, people who inherit wealth, on average, get richer faster than those who work for a living. In effect, the default trajectory is growing inequality. The only way that arrangement can be disrupted, Piketty indicates, is through state intervention. That was an important factor behind the growing equality in the United States during the three decades that followed World War II. Progressive tax rates and robust social welfare programs contributed to the most egalitarian *and* prosperous period in our history (see Frum 2000).

That some people who inherit wealth sometimes earn even more does not change the fact that the playing field is not fair. "I have inherited nothing," 2012 presidential candidate Mitt Romney proclaimed (Pareene 2012). For some reason he thought the million dollars of stocks his father left him did not count, probably because it constitutes such a small portion of his current holdings. Over time, he did secure an enormous fortune. Needless to say, though, a million-dollar start-up fund is hardly nothing, especially in the context of a low 15 percent capital gains tax. Not to mention the value of other forms of inherited capital, such as educational opportunities and social networks.

We might wonder if it matters that a few have much more than they need. When asked why he keeps giving public speeches, some of which pay up to a half million dollars, former president Bill Clinton said, "I gotta pay our bills" (Rucker 2015). Hillary Clinton explained that they were "dead broke" when they left the White House, with millions in legal debt, even though Bill Clinton made more than $18 million in speaking fees in the two years after he left office (Merica 2014). What is clear, though, is that some have less than they need. In 2013, the U.S. Census reported that 15 percent of Americans lived in poverty. That equals 45 million people. The poverty rate for children under 18 was 20 percent. This basic fact translates into inadequate food, lousy living conditions, poor health and dental care, inferior education, scarce access to computer technology, unsafe neighborhoods, meager job prospects, little political leverage, and limited legal recourse.

Something as fundamental as food has rippling implications. Inadequate nutrition translates into inadequate education, which leads to inadequate employment, which leads to inadequate food, and so on. More generally, new research demonstrates that the psychology of scarcity is burdensome indeed. It turns out that scarcity literally distracts the mind so significantly that it cannot pay attention to other matters. Thus food insecurity becomes psychological insecurity and intellectual insecurity (Mullainathan and Shafir 2013).

At a certain level—remember, one in five American kids is poor—this leads to societal insecurity. Why should a person who has only known scarcity—in terms of food, housing, health care, education, political influence, police protection—trust those in positions of authority? Taken one step further, why should leaders trust those who do not trust them? Why should affluent people trust poor people who do not trust them? And so on. At a certain level, scarcity tears apart the fabric of society.

In the most productive country in human history, however, material scarcity is far from inevitable. This is not only about fairness but also about care, because extreme affluence and extreme poverty are in fact linked. One issue here, contrary to even the most basic market logic, is that compensation and productivity have been decoupled. This has always been true in terms of wealth, which is largely distributed by way of inheritance. A child born into a rich family did nothing to earn his own wealth, just as a child born into a poor family did nothing to earn her own poverty—at least not when they started out (see Moriarty et al. 2012; Chetty et al. 2014).

Increasingly, though, the separation of pay from performance also applies to the "earned" income of adults, which has been beneficial to a few and harmful to many. "From 1978 to 2013," the Economic Policy Institute reports, "CEO compensation, inflation-adjusted, increased 937 percent, a rise more than double stock market growth and substantially greater than the painfully slow 10.2 percent growth in a typical worker's compensation over the same period" (A. Davis and Mishel 2014). Some people make less *because* others make more—not just because they add value. That is, if certain people are compensated above the aggregate level of productivity, that pay has to come from somewhere, which is to say a portion of the workforce has to be compensated below the average level of productivity. And it is not about performance, because some are paid more even when they are not productive. In many cases, including the recent recession and recovery, falling tides do not lower all boats and rising tides do not lift them.

A few still deny or downplay the facts of contemporary inequality (see, for example, Winship 2015; Rector and Sheffield 2011; Dorfman 2014). Many folks, however, are simply unaware of the extent of social inequality. For instance, most Americans imagine that wealth inequality is less extreme than it really is (Norton and Ariely 2011). Moreover, they think the distribution of wealth should be even more level than it is (Page and Jacobs 2009).

Likewise, few have full knowledge of how government-run social programs and tax policy tend to favor the affluent (Mettler 2010; Hacker and Pierson 2010). And many do not realize that the United States has some of the lowest tax rates in the industrialized world (Page and Jacobs 2009). The overall value of the retirement benefits exemption, health insurance exemption, and the mortgage interest deduction, all of which disproportionately help affluent families, far exceeds the combined value of food stamps, unemployment insurance, Temporary Assistance for Needy Families (TANF), and housing vouchers (Mettler 2011).

For anyone who genuinely studies the issues, it is clear that some have a lot more than others and that poverty is a very hard reality. Intentionally designed institutional and cultural arrangements reproduce this situation with some consistency.

The real debate is about our reactions to that, about the values and feelings we attach to such differences. To what extent is our level of social inequality acceptable? "I think if this country gets any kinder or gentler," Donald Trump declared in 1990, "it's literally going to cease to exist" (Plaskin 2016). Different countries make different choices—as the well-documented and highly variable rates of inequality across industrial nations illustrate. The real question is whether our current situation is aligned with our deepest sense of who we are as a society.

We still hear self-serving arguments that American poverty is not only OK but something to be celebrated. The richest member of Congress, Darrell Issa, asserted in 2015 that one of the things that makes America special is that "we have been able to make our poor somewhat the envy of the world" (Luhby 2015). In the same interview, he extolled the opportunity in America compared to third-world countries and suggests that if workers here want to be paid more they need to produce more. Aside from his funny use of the word *envy*, he compares apples to oranges and ignores the fact that the average American worker is being underpaid relative to productivity. It is also worth noting that the "opportunity" that makes us special has declined significantly in recent decades. Consequently, low-income families who are citizens in other industrial nations can count on more support and more opportunity than those in this country (Reeves 2014; Stiglitz 2015).

This acceptance of contemporary poverty may be a common view. It is certainly an opinion expressed frequently and forcefully by certain pundits and politicians. But such complacency is contrasted by the arguments of most experts and by the attitudes of the majority of citizens. Gallup reports that only 31 percent of Americans think money and wealth in the United States are distributed fairly. Some 63 percent believe money and wealth should be distributed more evenly (Newport 2015). Majorities of Republicans and Democrats alike support more progressive taxation to support government programs oriented toward education, childhood poverty, food insecurity, and health care (Page and Jacobs 2009).

Collectively, our practices generate an unnecessary and growing level of material insecurity, do not match our ideals, and represent real trouble in terms of the problem of care. If we do not care for the bodies of people, society is not viable.

WB: As we have just read, market ideology puts the squeeze on cheap labor in a way that seems sure to produce a permanent underclass of those who can never catch up (Berthoud 2010). While market ideology per se is a modern phenomenon, the practice of squeezing cheap labor is a very old and persistent problem. In ancient Israel, reflected in the Hebrew Bible/Old Testament, that "squeeze" featured interaction between peasant agricultural workers who lived in subsistence and the urban elites (kings, priests, scribes) who lived well from the surplus wealth appropriated from the produce of peasant labor.

The book of Deuteronomy is the great manifesto in

the Bible for socioeconomic, political justice. That tradition understood very well that unjust economic practices generated inequality that resulted in insecurity for the peasant producers of wealth. The tradition sets out to articulate an alternative economic vision that is theologically grounded (that is, grounded in what they took to be God's intention) in which the peasant producers of wealth and the elite beneficiaries of that wealth were perceived as "neighbors," people with a common stake in a viable economy that would generate material security for all participants. The tradition has a vivid memory of the exodus emancipation whereby the slaves of Pharaoh in Egypt who had been squeezed by Pharaoh for more production had been emancipated from that exploitative labor market by YHWH, the God of emancipation. That propelling memory for the tradition of Deuteronomy features both the memory of exploitation and the surge of emancipation. It is that double-pronged memory that permits the tradition of Deuteronomy to assert as motivation for an alternative economy, "Remember that you were a slave in the land of Egypt" (15:15; 16:12; 24:18, 22). Unsaid but clearly implied: and therefore act differently for the sake of the neighborhood so that such an economy of inequality does not again emerge in Israel.

The evoking crisis of what became a faith memory was the exploitation in Egypt. In Exodus 5 the "squeeze" by Pharaoh is repeatedly sounded as a summons to the slaves: "Make more bricks; make more bricks but gather your own supplies [straw]; go to your labors; you are lazy!" The rhetoric of reprimand of labor that does not produce enough sounds immediately contemporary to

us as the market ideology squeezes for more production.
The brutalizing production schedule of Pharaoh always
demands more. The way in which Israel remembers is
that the exploitative enterprise of Pharaoh was dramatically and decisively interrupted by YHWH, the God of
emancipation, who had heard the moans and groans of
the weary slaves (Exod. 2:23–25), who resolved to deliver
the slaves from oppression (3:7–9), and who dispatched
Moses as the human agent of deliverance (3:10). Thus
it is clear that this is a labor dispute that propels faith,
because YHWH, the God of emancipation, will not tolerate the gross inequality of Pharaoh and the slaves that
resulted in material security for Pharaoh at the expense
of the slaves who received from their labor no material
security at all.

With that backdrop, "Moses" is made, in the tradition, to be a defining agent for a revolutionary vision
of neighborliness that has concrete and specific implications for later economic practice and economic policy.
Here I will mention two regulations voiced by "Moses"
(here understood as the authorized voice of the tradition) on behalf of YHWH that seek to transpose the
memory of deliverance into continuing economic practice. The social relationships of later generations are to
be informed by this defining memory of exploitation
and emancipation. In Deuteronomy 24:14–15 the teaching of Moses requires prompt payment to laborers:

> You shall not withhold the wages of poor and needy
> laborers, whether other Israelites or aliens who reside
> in your land in one of your towns. You shall pay them
> their wages daily before sunset, because they are poor
> and their livelihood depends on them; otherwise they

might cry to the LORD against you, and you would
incur guilt.

The regulation assumes that workers were receiving wages, so we are already dealing with a wage-based
economy. Notably the regulation pertains alike to Israelites and "aliens," a term that might be translated as
"immigrant." All laborers are treated as belonging to a
single group, as they certainly are in economic terms,
thus deserving fair treatment, as they are all vulnerable.
What they have in common, Israelite and "alien," is that
they are dependent upon their regular wage payments
for their work. The situation of Moses, moreover, concerns the "poor and needy" laborers, those who have no
surplus at all but who live from wage payment to wage
payment. The prohibition is against "withholding"
wages. As we know, there are many ways of withholding wages, all of which, from the perception of the poor,
amount to wage theft. The employers, if they are ruthless enough and care only about the squeeze of productivity and profit, might withhold for taxes, for medical
benefits, for parking, or a dozen other reasons that must
come "out of wages" and not "out of profits." Specifically the regulation concerns delayed payment. It was
surely known, already then, that if an employer can
report that "the check is in the mail," or can otherwise
delay payment, he can make good use and good profit
from the withheld wages, even for a brief time. Thus the
regulation is exactly a defense of the vulnerable laborer
against exploitative employers, because such practice of
withholding wages will enhance the material security of
the employer at the expense of the worker.

The regulation is reinforced by the motivational clause that alludes to the attentiveness of YHWH, who monitors the economy. In the tradition of Deuteronomy it is known from the outset that YHWH is peculiarly attentive to the cries of exploited labor, and that such cries of anguish and protest can mobilize God against the exploiter. The book of Deuteronomy wants to recall the destruction of Pharaoh and his production system as a threat against employers who continue to perform the role of Pharaoh in their brutalizing production requirements. That citation of YHWH is a signal that the tradition of Deuteronomy (and indeed of ancient Israel generally) is that economic practice is *not* a zone of autonomy in which the powerful are free to do what they want. Even economic practices are situated in a world where the intention of the creator God is operative. In a market ideology, an allusion to YHWH the creator God of the exodus might not carry much freight. Deuteronomy, however, insists that the production narrative by itself is no adequate way to understand economic issues. Its inadequacy is that it fails to recognize that laborers are in fact human agents who are intrinsically entitled by the ordering of creation to dignity, respect, and the wherewithal for a viable life. Thus the seemingly small act of withholding wages, even for a day, is linked to a larger vision of neighborliness that cannot be violated with impunity. It is the God of the exodus, in the horizon of Israel, who continues to occupy economic arrangements. Practice and policy that violate what is known of this emancipatory God are sure to end in failure and eventually in big trouble of a destructive kind.

In the regulation that precedes this one in Deuteronomy 24:10–13, Moses declares:

> When you make your neighbor a loan of any kind, you shall not go into the house to take the pledge. You shall wait outside, while the person to whom you are making the loan brings the pledge out to you. If the person is poor, you shall not sleep in the garment given you as the pledge. You shall give the pledge back by sunset, so that your neighbor may sleep in the cloak and bless you; and it will be to your credit before the LORD your God.

It is as if Moses understood that credit and loans are not only at the center of the economy, but also at the center of a viable human community. The assumption, so easy for us, that one has enough resources to make a loan or one has needs and no resources, is already a signal of a certain arrangement of social equilibrium. For that reason, how the creditor who has all the leverage acts with reference to the debtor who has no leverage at all matters to the health of society and here matters to the God who is Lord of creditors and debtors. Thus the large theological claims of the God of the exodus are brought to bear specifically on a concrete economic transaction. In the world of the market narrative, the transaction seems normal and requires some collateral to secure the loan. Set in the exodus narrative, however, the transaction is of immense social importance and therefore must be done correctly, because everything is at stake in the transaction for the well-being of society.

The question raised in every transaction of credit and debt concerns collateral (here given as "pledge").

The first prohibition of the regulation is against seizure of the collateral item by intrusion into the safe place of the potential debtor. In a usurpatious economy, creditors tend to have all the leverage of law on their side, and so are free to transgress the boundaries of neighborliness in the interest of economic advantage. But here such economic leverage is limited, because the debtor has certain inviolate rights that must be respected. As those rights are respected, so the person of the potential debtor is respected.

But the second stipulation in verse 12 is even more specific. Here the object of consideration is the potential debtor who is poor. Because a poor person likely has little to offer as collateral, it is imagined that the poor person might offer a coat as collateral; indeed, if desperate enough, he might offer the only coat he has. It is that single coat that would be the only cover a poor person might have at night. The regulation, oddly enough, permits the taking of the single coat of a poor debtor as collateral. But then it requires that the coat be returned to the debtor at sunset, that is, when it gets cold, as needed for safe, warm sleep. The debtor is vulnerable and might die in the cold of the night. This provision thus voices an almost comic scene of a banker going each morning to the house of the poor debtor to pick up collateral to keep all day, and each evening returning it to the house of the debtor for the safe, warm sleep of the debtor. Such a daily practice would indicate that the collateral is not very "secure." More than that, the process is immensely inconvenient: imagine picking up the coat as collateral and returning it every day on a thirty-year loan! Likely the intent of the regulation is to make the process so inconvenient that the creditor will simply forgo collateral and let the poor debtor keep the coat, day and night.

The regulation ends now with an affirmation of the creditor who faithfully manages the collateral. The debtor might well bless such a creditor, that is, thank him and be grateful. Thus an economic transaction has been transposed into a neighborly transaction. Because the creditor recognizes the human face of the debtor as a neighbor, the debtor can recognize the human face of the creditor and be grateful. The final element of the regulation suggests that the creditor receives additional "credit" with the God of the exodus. The concluding statement suggests that even the creditor is a debtor before the creator God, who has all the resources. As the creditor has genuinely allowed credit to the debtor, so God extends credit to the creditor, who is in fact a debtor before God. This final phrasing destabilizes roles that would be taken for granted in ordinary economic terms: the debtor is one who makes credit possible for the creditor, and the creditor turns out to be a debtor in need of credit. When the roles are destabilized, there is a chance for neighborliness that extends well beyond defined economic roles.

If we consider these two commandments together (Deut. 24:10–13, 14–15), we may observe two matters. First, the motivational clauses are very different in the two cases. In verse 13, the motivational clause is positive: practice this and be blessed! In verse 15, by contrast, the motivation is negative; failure to practice what

is required is surely to "incur guilt." The two motivations go together and might have been reversed in the
two cases. Economic transactions are in fact venues in
which either blessing or guilt is a potential outcome.
Attention must be paid to the way in which economic
transactions are defined and implemented as neighborly
processes. In the first case, the creditor and the debtor
are "neighbors." In the second, the laborer and the
employer are neighbors. Both relationships are in the
world of YHWH, who blesses and judges.

The second observation is that, in both cases, the
limit for action is "sunset." The laws assume and voice
a distinct difference between day and night as zones
of economic transaction and neighborly equity. Before
sunset, the reality of wages, credit, and collateral pertains. But at sunset, these categories cease to operate. At
sunset, no more withholding of collateral. At sunset, no
more withholding of wages. No more credit and no more
withholding at sunset; the categories of the market cease
to operate and neighborliness becomes the appropriate
and required mode of relationships. Such a limit that is
nonnegotiable is a mighty curb against acquisitiveness.
The pause of sunset is the recognition and embrace of
neighborliness as the defining reality of human transaction. Thus the psalmist can observe the rhythms of life
ordained by the Creator:

> You make darkness, and it is night,
>   when all the animals of the forest come creeping out.
> The young lions roar for their prey,
>   seeking their food from God.
> When the sun rises, they withdraw

and lie down in their dens.
People go out to their work
and to their labor until the evening.
                    (Ps. 104:20–23)

The darkness is dangerous when the lions prowl. It is a time for neighborly solidarity that overrides all of the economic distinctions and inequities of the day.

The memory of the exodus led in the Bible to an enduring awareness of the squeeze of labor and the inequality that made it possible and that generated even greater inequality. The Bible, of course, does more than narrate an awareness of that inequality. It aims to redress that inequality and to summon those in subsistence and those in surplus to a common good. It intends that redress both as social practice and as social policy. But it also insists that such social efforts are grounded in the intention of YHWH, the God of emancipation. That God turns up, in the rhetoric of ancient Israel, not as an idea but as a practice. The clearest articulation of YHWH as practice is found in the poetic utterance of Jeremiah 22:13–18. The poem begins with a critical assault on the king, Jehoiakim, who is regarded as a self-indulgent abuser of workers:

Woe to him who builds his house by unrighteousness,
    and his upper rooms by injustice;
who makes his neighbors work for nothing,
    and does not give them their wages;
who says, "I will build myself a spacious house
    with large upper rooms,"
and who cuts out windows for it,
    paneling it with cedar,
    and painting it with vermilion.

Are you a king
  because you compete in cedar?
                    (vv, 13–15a)

The introductory "woe" is a declaration that big trouble will come on the royal system of abuse. The specificity of abuse is unrighteousness and injustice that takes the form of labor exploitation. The laborers are identified as "neighbors" of the king, though of course the king does not imagine them as neighbors, but only as performers of necessary tasks that enhance royal splendor. The king enjoys the luxury of spaciousness, windows, cedar, and vermilion, all evidences of advantages available only to those who enjoy cheap labor and surplus wealth. Thus the exploited "neighbors" not only do labor but also pay the taxes that support the elite enterprise of royalty. The king is accused of dishonest gain, shedding innocent blood (a figure of dehumanizing exploitation), the practice of oppression, and violence. This is a description of a predatory economy!

Such predation, says the poem, can only lead to a dishonorable death:

They shall not lament for him, saying,
  "Alas, my brother!" or "Alas, sister!"
They shall not lament for him, saying,
  "Alas, lord!" or "Alas, his majesty!"
With the burial of a donkey he shall be buried—
  dragged off and thrown out beyond the gates of
    Jerusalem.
                    (vv. 18–19)

No tears will be shed for such an exploiter!
Between the initial indictment of the self-indulgent

king (vv. 13–15a) and the anticipation of his ignoble death (vv. 18–19), the poem pauses to entertain an alternative to this rapaciousness:

> Did not your father eat and drink
>   and do justice and righteousness?
> Then it was well with him.
> He judged the cause of the poor and needy;
>   then it was well.
> Is not this to know me?
>   says the LORD.
>
> (vv. 15b–16)

The reference is to Josiah, the good king who preceded Jehoiakim on the throne. He is remembered as a king of sound social policy (justice and righteousness) that contrasts with the unrighteousness and injustice of his son. This remembered king "ate and drank," that is, lived a good life and prospered. He "judged" (that is, maintained justice) for the poor and needy, the very ones whom his son used abusively, and therefore he prospered.

Most astonishing is the last line of verse 16 wherein YHWH is referenced as saying: "Is not this to know me?" This spectacular statement does not say that "knowledge of God" will lead to care for the poor and the needy. Nor does it say that care for the poor and needy will lead to "knowledge of God." Rather it equates *knowledge of God* with *care for the poor and needy*. Such attentiveness to the neighbors is itself an awareness of and embrace of God. Thus God is not an abstract idea or a holy presence remote from issues of equality and material security. Rather God is seen to be an agency, presence, and interaction who dwells amid the very processes of neighborly justice that curb inequality. Such a remarkable equation completely recharacterizes God as a process of neighborly activity. But it also recharacterizes the neighborly processes of economic justice as having transcendent significance and urgency. The outcome in this prophetic insistence is that material security and equality are not incidental by-products of faith in the orbit of ancient Israel. Economic transactions constitute the very venue in which the ultimate truth of the world is disclosed. This remarkable claim is grounded in the exodus memory, where God is shown to be the overthrower of injustice and the generator of neighborliness that allows there to be a later recognition that *love of God* can only be articulated as *love of neighbor*:

> Those who say, "I love God," and hate their brothers or sisters, are liars; for those who do not love a brother or sister whom they have seen, cannot love God whom they have not seen. The commandment we have from him is this: those who love God must love their brothers and sisters also. (1 John 4:20–21)

The text here speaks of "brothers and sisters." The Old Testament prefers "neighbors." But they are the same. Both speak of all members of the society. The predatory economy likes to pretend that we have no neighbors or brothers or sisters, only rivals, competitors, and threats. The teaching of the Bible is an insistence that such an assumption of the predatory economy is false and cannot be sustained. That it is false and unsustainable is always being rediscovered by some contemporary pharaoh. Like the original pharaoh, however, it is characteristically rediscovered too late. In every generation, witnesses to the contrary always consider how late it is, and whether it is a time to opt for neighborliness as social policy and practice.

Chapter 2

FAIRNESS

JB: MY EARLIEST, MOST VIVID MEMORY OF SYSTEMATIC injustice was the Pinewood Derby. I did not know at the time that my particular ordeal with Cub Scout Pack 306 was part and parcel of this annual American tradition (*Reader's Digest* 2006). I made my own car. Unlike most of the other boys, including all those with a car that was remotely competitive, I was on my own. My dad had neither the tools, skill, nor inclination to help me. I guess I had not put a huge amount of effort into my car, but as a fourth-grader it was more time than I had spent on almost anything else to date.

When I arrived at the race that evening with cautiously high hopes, it was immediately obvious to me and everybody else on hand that my car was outclassed. Over the course of the next couple of hours (first impressions

proved accurate: my car was ugly and slow by comparison), I brooded on the lessons. In particular, my dad was
flawed, my Scout troop was crummy, and I was lame;
more generally, nice guys finish last, and adults do not
always follow the rules either. To this day, I remember
what my car looked like and what the best cars looked
like. And I remember that this evening of lies put into
question all the other claims the leaders of Pack 306 had
made. I did not remain a Scout for long. Perhaps I knew
that I was facing a basic strain in the human experience,
the problem of fairness.

This category relates to the first, but whereas the
problem of care is mostly an issue of material security,
the problem of fairness is mostly a matter of relative
comparison. Is everyone doing their share? Is anyone
getting something for nothing? Is everyone getting what
they deserve?

The key to this moral foundation is social buy-in.
There is no single way to be fair. Rather, members of
society must perceive that the rules of the system are
reasonable in the first place and are being applied in a
way that is just. ("Here is a piece of wood, some wheels,
and nails; make a car with them!")

For a lot of us the problem of fairness is not an
abstract, philosophical question, but rather an immediate, daily, lived experience. It is about siblings, spouses,
coworkers, and neighbors. Are they dealing with me in a
reasonable manner? It is about leadership—and followership. That is, are leaders setting sensible rules and following the rules they themselves enforce? Do followers
make such possibilities plausible?

While it is largely a matter of perception—it is

whether people regard an arrangement as legitimate that counts—there is still something elemental here. Human society is predicated on the idea that there is something that binds "us" together. It is not simply common biology or mutual self-interest codified in a contract, but what Émile Durkheim calls the "properly social."

"Men cannot live together," he argues, "without agreeing, and consequently without making mutual sacrifices, joining themselves to one another in a strong and enduring fashion. Every society is a moral society" (Durkheim 1997, 173). Every society that lasts, at least. It requires shared meaning, that is, culture. A culture is only viable if enough people think its norms make sense.

There is an influential body of research in criminology extending from Durkheim and developed by Robert Merton known as strain theory (see Agnew 1995). According to this school of thought, society needs to communicate clear, constructive goals to its members and then provide them with the means to achieve those objectives. Without such goals, deviant behavior is more likely. If the goals are communicated but the means of achieving them are not made available, the result is social strain. And strain raises the chances of delinquency. Imagine being told you can do anything you want because "the American dream offers expansive opportunity," but living in a setting with terrible schools and few job opportunities.

In general, according to this logic, parents, teachers, clergy, journalists, business leaders, and others in positions of authority have to help communicate the value of working hard, respecting laws, taking care of children, and making useful contributions to our civic life.

Such institutional leaders also have to make sure that the experience of all Americans includes sound education and effective socialization processes for kids, solid employment opportunities that utilize the skills young people learn in school, safe housing, healthy food, and political representation. When the chains linking people to these resources falter, we can expect that some will not "buy in." When the goals of such achievement are relentlessly promoted but the means are not obtainable, the strain that results could entail a sense that things are not fair.

According to the perspective, this incongruity explains a wide range of crimes related to delinquency (see Agnew 1992; 2006; Messner and Rosenfeld 1994). In the criminological research derived from strain theory, the focus is on how these dynamics affect various crime rates. But it is conceivable that the same logic applies more widely. If the system does not work, if some people believe that the social covenant of society is fractured, it is easy to imagine how they would act out.

More generally, we know that that extreme inequality fosters distrust, which makes the basic functioning of social institutions such as government, education, and criminal justice more precarious (Wilkinson and Pickett 2009). It negatively affects subjective feelings like happiness (Oishi, Kesebir, and Diener 2011; Oishi, Schimmack, and Diener 2012), objective well-being or mortality (Lynch et al. 1998), as well as collective welfare, political stability, and economic growth (Soubbotina and Sheram 2000). Perhaps this also helps account for the epidemic of rudeness, uncivil behavior at work and in public places, and the growing resentment directed toward elite institutional leaders (see Paxton 2005; Pearson and Porath 2005; Truss 2005; Carter 1998).

Lots of signs indicate that something is broken in this regard. Not just the extraordinary presidential campaign of Donald Trump, but analytical evidence shows that the baseline level of distrust for the most influential insiders is staggering. Recent Gallup numbers show that Americans' confidence in different branches of the federal government has reached record lows. Just 7 percent have confidence in Congress.

A serious problem was made worse by the Supreme Court's ruling in *Citizens United v. Federal Election Commission*, which allowed even greater amounts of money to flow throughout the political system (Tribe and Matz 2014). The hallowed and freighted tradition of "one person, one vote" is giving way to "one dollar, one vote," and thereby undermining the foundational ideals of democracy. Hidden donations, tax loopholes, lobbying, false advertising, and untruthful political rhetoric all foster public cynicism (see Dorgan 2006).

Many lower- and middle-class families feel they have to work harder to maintain their quality of life relative to changes in the cost of living, while concentrated wealth in the hands of the upper class becomes more extreme every year (see Schor 2004; Kalleberg 2009; Pugh 2009). Growing gaps in education, a decimated labor movement, tax structure and loopholes that favor the wealthy all help reproduce and intensify income inequality—and contradict the spirit of the American dream.

Large corporations have obviously achieved great things. Firms like Eli Lilly, Microsoft, Hasbro, and Xerox are known for responsible corporate citizenship and making a lot of products that people want and need. The complexity and scale of corporate production makes it hard for small firms to do the same thing. At the same time, there is growing perception that multinational corporations do not play by the same rules as everyone else. Monopolistic or oligopolistic industries unchecked by regulation are especially problematic. Health care, meat processing, and computer hardware companies, for example, have all earned the criticism they have received in this regard.

On a good day, according to market logic, a firm should maximize the investment of its shareholders. That does not take into account broader concerns like the interests of the community, nation, or environment. Plus, on a bad day, corporate leaders do not always put the interests of shareholders up front. Lack of transparency, exclusive corporate governance, jacked-up prices, wage theft, insider trading, destructive environmental impact, exorbitant executive pay, bonuses unconnected to performance, bonuses on the heels of government bailouts, and surreptitious data mining have become the new normal (Kuttner 1999; Bobo 2009; Sandel 2012; Buchheit 2013).

We sometimes imagine that greater morality leads to more material success. "Early to bed and early to rise," Benjamin Franklin advised, "makes a man healthy, wealthy, and wise." This was the logic of the original Protestant ethic described by Max Weber. And isn't it how the American dream works?

Not anymore. Intergenerational mobility has stagnated. Recent studies indicate that skepticism about those at the top may be warranted. Indeed, contrary to common stereotypes, a growing body of research suggests that upper-class individuals are more likely to behave unethically than lower-class individuals (see Piff et al. 2012). One of the conclusions in this research is that the motivation of greed serves the goal of wealth, but not that of wisdom.

Not surprisingly, perhaps, Americans' trust of top executives is thinning (see the Edelman Trust Barometer 2015). The outrage over CEO compensation is relevant here too. In this instance, it appears that Americans' frustration may not be related to the market affording top executives too much pay. Drawing from old philosophical traditions that can be traced back to John Locke and Adam Smith, most Americans have always been comfortable with lots of money being paid to people who *earn* it. The exasperation on the part of many is that the highest levels of corporate compensation are not based on performance in the market, as noted above. Extra pay that is unconnected to productivity is built into contracts. The $28.5 million in bonuses received by Wall Street executives in 2014, for example, represents a 3 percent increase from the prior year, even though industry profits declined 4.5 percent (Anderson 2015; see also Owen 2009; Sweet 2014). Again, the normal rules do not apply. Or more to the point, elite managers get to make their own rules. Carly Fiorina helped lay off tens of thousands of Hewlett-Packard employees and diminish the value of the company's stock by half, pocketed more than $100 million along the way, and then somehow attempted to run a presidential campaign on that record. Some would call it hubris. But she calls it "the face of leadership," and many agree.

"We don't have to choose between capitalism and fairness," warns Joseph Stiglitz. "We must choose both" (2015, 131). Whether reining in such excessive executive compensation will ultimately alter the American stratification system is far from settled. What is not in question, though, is that the status quo is part of a larger mess relative to the problem of fairness. The rhetoric of the American dream increasingly sounds ironic. A culture that persistently teaches people to make a certain contribution to their society and expect corresponding rewards for such efforts, and then does not provide the means for achieving those goals, is not sustainable. A society that maintains this contradiction while passively watching leaders hoard resources invites unrest. The predictable result is, at best, a certain malaise. Perhaps an epidemic of rudeness and incivility and loss of faith in leaders fits the bill. At worst? Disengagement, defiance, protest, and violence. Maybe this paradox motivated the Occupy Movement or the rage so many feel toward the police. But anyone who thinks it cannot get much worse is not paying attention.

WB: WHEN THE MARKET "DEVELOPS" FROM AN exchange mechanism to a regulative principle for all social relationships, it begins to operate by its own logic and rules without reference or accountability to the social fabric in which it is embedded (Berthoud 2010). Certainly the market—and market logic—are complex, but we may summarize what appear to be the guidelines or rules for the claims of market ideology:

1. The market operates in an economy of scarcity that evokes bottomless anxiety. Thus economics courses

under the aegis of that ideology operate from the premise that economics is the "study of the distribution of scarce goods." Because goods are said to be scarce, there is a performed anxiety about having enough, about getting "my fair share," and about getting as much of the neighbor's share as is possible.

2. Anxiety about scarcity propels a lust for more. Thus the economy must continue to "grow," and the predatory takers are propelled to take as much as they can. That lust for more eventually is no longer informed by need or even by realistic want, but takes on a life of its own, of taking for the sake of taking. The health of the market depends upon generating more needs so that we can be supplied with things that we did not know we needed.

3. Anything and everything, and eventually everyone, is a tradable commodity that can be had for a price. When everything and everyone is reduced to a commodity, other values begin to lose their force and their attractiveness. For example, on the *Antiques Road Show*, there is little interest in the object of art; we are dazzled only by the dollar amount that can be assigned to the object.

4. As other values diminish in attractiveness and compelling force, every and any action becomes justifiable, as long as it serves the acquisition of scarce goods. There is no moral norm outside of "more" by which to test actions of acquisitiveness. As a result we witness in big finance no reluctance except for "getting caught," thus an absence of moral restraint or of moral imagination.

5. Market logic that justifies the lust for more is designed to be confiscatory. It is not confiscatory by

happenstance—that is its purpose. Unrestrained acquisitiveness treats any object or any person as a candidate
for confiscatory effort.

6. This lust for acquisition requires the disregard
of the neighbor, whose presence no longer restrains,
because the other is not perceived as a neighbor but only
as a threat or as a competitor for scarce goods. The outcome of the disposal of the neighbor is the forfeiture of
the common good that requires endless investment for
maintenance and nurture. Thus we witness the demise
of a viable social infrastructure in an economy of unrestrained greed.

This market ideology is a modern phenomenon
commonly attributed to the formulations of Adam
Smith, who had behind him the rational autonomy of
René Descartes. This entire modern trajectory through
the work of Milton Friedman has been an endless and
indefatigable adversarial stance toward the restraints
of tradition and community that might provide norms
of restraint for acquisitiveness. To that extent, market
ideology as a justification of acquisitiveness is a modern program. But the phenomenon of greedy acquisitiveness at the expense of the common good and at the
disregard of the neighbor is not a modern problem. It is
a key preoccupation of the Old Testament, even if economic matters are framed somewhat differently. In that
ancient world the economy consisted of an ongoing tension between the agricultural peasant economy of the
village and the surplus economy of the city of Jerusalem (Adams 2014; Boer 2015). In that context, the Old
Testament offers vigorous voices that speak with robust
critique of the predatory economy of the urban elites

and that champion an alternative economy of neighborliness that resists "the logic of the market" and the ways
in which it puts the human infrastructure in jeopardy.
The way in which these poetic figures frame the matter
is an insistence that YHWH, the God of exodus emancipation and the Lord of the covenant, finds the predatory
economy intolerable. It is important that these critical
voices are characteristically expressed in poetic image
and metaphor, because such speech refuses reduction to
predictable prose, to manageable mantras and slogans,
or to one-dimensional social analysis. The rhetoric of
these forceful critics intends to disrupt the numbness of
the predatory economy and its practitioners.

I will cite three exemplary texts from these poetic
figures who dissent from the dominant economy and its
logic of commodity. In Amos 8:4–8 the poem begins with
an imperative "hear" (*shema'*) that echoes the ancient
summons of the Torah (famously Deut. 6:4). That is, the
practitioners of the predatory economy are addressed
and called to account, an address that we would have
thought the economy had effectively screened out. We
may notice five accents in this brief poem from Amos
that together constitute a major assault on the economics of unrestrained greed:

1. The ones addressed (but not tamed) prey on the
vulnerable, here as in many places, "the needy and the
poor." These are the peasants who are economically vulnerable, who have little social power, who operate without surplus, and who are readily "brought to ruin" by
the manipulations of the market economy. The needy
and poor are simply an inconvenience in the way of
aggressive commerce and count for nothing in their

vulnerability. More than that, the prophetic tradition is characteristically in solidarity with these vulnerable subjects of predation.

2. Those who are propelled by a lust for more are impatient with the traditional pauses for sociability. The poet mentions two specific festivals, "new moon" and "sabbath." Sabbath occurs with weekly frequency. "New moon" is a recurrent festival according to the phases of the moon. Both the weekly and the monthly social observances required a pause that was inconvenient for commerce. These occasions provided a time for leisurely social interaction, perhaps some religious-moral reflection on social practice, and a cessation of trade. We may imagine that those here addressed were restless amid such a required restfulness and watched the clock for the time when they could return to their aggressive hustle. As we witness the encroachment of the market on such holidays as Thanksgiving, with stores open earlier and earlier, and we observe the total collapse of Sunday as a traditional day of rest, we do not need much imagination to see that the traders addressed in this ancient poetry had no appreciation for a social provision that was freighted with symbolic significance.

3. Those addressed are accused of skewing fair trade by intentionally using dishonest arrangements in the selling of goods. While the exact measure of "ephah" and "shekel" is obscure for us, the point is clear enough. Rigged scales mean dishonest transactions in which the needy and the poor are victims of intentional exploitation. It is not a far leap from this rhetoric to payday lenders, hidden interest costs on loans, and the ways in which sharp dealings do in the innocent and the unsuspecting,

or the suspecting who have no leverage against such a system.

In the ancient Torah of Moses, the use of honest weights is required:

> You shall not have in your bag two kinds of weights, large and small. You shall not have in your house two kinds of measures, large and small. You shall have only a full and honest weight; you shall have only a full and honest measure, so that your days may be long in the land that the LORD your God is giving you. For all who do such things, all who act dishonestly, are abhorrent to the LORD your God. (Deut. 25:13–16)

This means that crooked scales are not only an affront to the neighbor, but an affront to the Lord God. Such a practice is said to be "abhorrent" to God; a stronger translation might be "abomination," a word used to characterize what so deeply repels YHWH that YHWH will not remain in such an environment. Thus a crooked weight or measure jeopardizes the divine presence, which is definitional for the community. A withdrawal of such divine presence may entail the loss of the land; here the matter is voiced positively: divine presence permits being "long in the land." Thus Israel characteristically finds deep urgency in small economic practices. Such a connection is not unlike a "broken glass" theory of crime in which a small violation may lead to great risk. The risk to well-being will show up in the most mundane of neighborly transactions.

4. The poor are turned into a commodity for negotiation in trade. This poem suggests that the poor are purchasable for shoes. The needy are equivalent to a

pair of sandals. Everyone has a price, and the price of the poor and the needy is very low. The same rhetoric is used in Amos 2:6–7, where the poor are reduced to a cheap price.

5. The deep indignation of the poem comes to fruition in verses 7–8. The poet not only imagines that such dishonest actions have social consequences, but beyond that, the Lord—the emancipator from Egypt and its predatory economy—is a witness to the logic of commodity. YHWH will never forget! The rhetoric insists that there is a transcendent significance to this abusive conduct that has outcomes that are guaranteed in the name of this God. The language remains poetic. The operative words are *tremble* and *mourn*. The land will tremble in fear; the people will mourn at loss. Without specificity the poet declares that this seemingly petty violation of the vulnerable neighbor by dishonest weights has unavoidable cosmic implications.

The poem ends with images of a seething disorder and restless turmoil that is not unlike the churning of the Nile River. Thus the seething, surging trouble cannot be contained or managed any more than the Nile can be tamed at flood stage. The risk that the poet discerns in such commodity logic that was on exhibit in ancient Israel does not lead to "prophetic prediction." It leads rather to an emotive attempt to penetrate the numb indifference of market practitioners. Such rhetoric refuses the logic of the market. There is here no cause and effect other than an insistence that the ultimacy of God be taken seriously in the affairs of the market. If we were to attempt to identify such seething disorder and restless turmoil in our time unleashed by such

today

antineighborly logic, we might point to the social unrest and its extreme expression in "terrorism." Or we might consider the environmental threat that has been, at least in part, evoked by fossil fuels mobilized in a system of greed. The poetry intends that those who hear it should experience, in the poetic act, significant destabilization; that poetic destabilization is matched by dislocation that happens in the real world when neighborliness is reduced to traffic commodities.

In Micah, a later contemporary of Amos, we get a not dissimilar poem:

> Alas for those who devise wickedness
>   and evil deeds on their beds!
> When the morning dawns, they perform it,
>   because it is in their power.
> They covet fields, and seize them;
>   houses, and take them away;
> they oppress householder and house.
>   people and their inheritance.
> Therefore thus says the LORD:
> Now, I am devising against this family an evil
>   from which you cannot remove your necks;
> and you shall not walk haughtily,
>   for it will be an evil time.
> On that day they shall take up a taunt song against you,
>   and wail with bitter lamentation,
> and say, "We are utterly ruined;
>   the LORD alters the inheritance of my people;
> how he removes it from me!
>   Among our captors he parcels out our fields."
> Therefore you will have no one to cast the line by lot
>   in the assembly of the LORD.   (2:1–5)

This remarkable poem contains the usual elements of a prophetic speech of judgment. It describes the way in which Israel has violated torah and offended

YHWH. In verses 1–2 the indictment of Israel concerns an act of coveting. The allusion to the tenth commandment of Sinai, "You shall not covet," is unmistakable (Exod. 20:17). The act of coveting consists in two elements. First, there is the desire, wanting what belongs to another. Second, there is an act of seizure of what belongs to another. The desire, says Micah, happens in the night, scheming while they are in bed. They can plan and scheme in the dark of night. Then when the sun comes up, they move into action and implement their desire and seize the houses and fields of others. The seizure is likely not violent. It is rather through land speculation, legal cunning, and management of credit, loans, and interest. The outcome is the displacement of neighbors. The final term of the indictment in verse 2, "inheritance," bespeaks old tribal or village land that has belonged forever by custom to a family. And now it is lost in sharp dealing, not unlike the land of the Okies in Steinbeck's *Grapes of Wrath*.

The divine punishment of such a violation of the neighborhood is initiated with "alas" ("woe"). It means "big sadness to come." Big trouble is to come upon the acquisitive. The poet voices the resolve of God to enforce God's prohibition ("You shall not covet") and to punish those who violate. The prophetic voices in Israel regularly insist that the proprieties of decent neighborliness are guaranteed by God, who monitors the economic life of the community. The punishment that is anticipated is exactly commensurate with the offense. Now the land of the speculators will be lost. They had seized the land of others; now their land will be seized. It will not be lost by direct divine intervention, but through an invading force. Thus the phrase "not remove your necks" likely refers to a yoke of taxes imposed by a foreign occupier. The poet anticipates that God (!) "parcels out our fields" among "our captors" (in context, the Assyrian army). The whole narrative concerns the threat of military occupations. Those who took the "inheritance" of others (v. 2) in time to come will lose their "inheritance" (v. 4). And it is all, says the poet, the work of God.

The poet further anticipates the response of the ruthless land speculators from verses 1–2 who will now speak out, shocked and sad, as they did not see it coming. They will utter vigorous complaints against God (v. 4). Indeed, the poet can even imagine what they will say in their deep loss. They will weep in their loss. They will accuse God of changing the rules concerning the land of promise to which they thought they had abiding title. They will describe how the occupying army now enjoys their land. The poem appeals, in advance, to a deep level of pain and pathos that is sure to come. Micah's listeners had not yet seen the future they had chosen for themselves. But he invites them to imagine their future. And the reason he (and they) may imagine such a future is because coveting has been prohibited by God. There is a high price to pay for such a violation.

In his final verse of the poem, the poet anticipates the "assembly," the town meeting when the land is reapportioned according to new political circumstance as the rules of property are changed. He anticipates that the ones whom he addresses will not be given admission or representation in the meeting. Without representation they will end with no land at the conclusion of the meeting. They will end in utter displacement and dismay, foiled completely in their attempt to have land that did not belong to them. Land seizure cannot be done with impunity; there is a high price to pay!

We should not be misled by the spectacular rhetoric that the poet places in God's mouth. God is, in the rhetoric, the invisible connection between the violation of neighborliness and the future of those who violate. But the future of the entire narrative is accomplished by an invading military force, not by God's direct action. Thus we may imagine a surplus economy that is so corrupt and exploitative and therefore weak that it is lacking in solidarity that is necessary for its sustenance and protection. The effect of the poem is to affirm that the much-enjoyed prosperity of the present is unsustainable, because it is anti-neighborly. There is an accountability for anti-neighborliness that cannot be eluded. This is a song about that inescapable accountability.

In a much later text, the poet in Isaiah 58:1–9 critiques a self-complacent community of pious folk who love their religious activity. They are so committed to it that they can imagine that their worship should assure them well-being. But, says the poet, showy religion cannot cover for shabby abusive economics. In verse 2 the poet employs the most familiar word pair of the prophets, "righteousness" and "justice" (NRSV "ordinance"). These pious folk have not obeyed the Torah and have not cared about the common good. In verse 3 the poet becomes quite specific about the failure of such phony piety:

They are preoccupied with such surface matter as religious fast days that have no real seriousness for them. This sounds like a counterpoint to the folks in the poetry of

Amos who watched their clocks in order to get back to
commerce as soon as possible. Here their religion has
screened out all economic issues.

They have oppressed their workers! This is perhaps the
ur-sin in Israel's prophetic faith. That faith is preoccupied
with neighborly justice issues and knows that the key to
such justice—and the source of social well-being—is fair
play toward vulnerable workers who have no surplus but
who depend on what they earn. This prophetic passion
no doubt goes back to the memory of the exodus when
Pharaoh oppressed his workers, who are the ancestors
in Isaiah's address. And if the matter reaches back as far
as Pharaoh, we can see that the agenda reaches forward
even to our own time, in which a minimum wage in our
society means living at poverty level and in which production schedules squeeze more and more work from
workers who have fewer and fewer rights and protection.
Thus Karl Marx was surely right in his aphorism:

> The criticism of heaven is thus transformed into the
>   criticism of earth,
> The criticism of religion into the criticism of law,
> And the criticism of theology into the criticism of
>   politics.
>   (quoted in McLellan 1971, 22)

Except Isaiah, long before Marx, works it from the
other end so that the criticism of *religion* becomes the criticism of *economics*. Isaiah has begun by a critique of their
surface piety; but it morphed into a critique of *economic
practice*. The two are intimately related to each other.
The poem begins with an exposé of religion that needs
to ask about economics; the faithful are summoned to

an attentive economics. And then, in a more familiar passage, the poet prescribes an alternative action to be undertaken by the pious as a real fast:

— set the oppressed free from "every yoke" of coercion
— provide bread
— provide housing
— provide clothing

Religion is redefined as neighborly economics.

And from neighborly generous economics, we get, in verses 8–9, a double "then" of consequences:

> *Then* the light of divine presence and human well-being will dawn.
> *Then* God will answer when Israel calls in need.

But not until *then*! There will be right relations with God when there are right relations with neighbor!

The poems of Amos, Micah, and the later Isaiah, along with many other prophetic poems, attest that the God of this tradition has a relentless insistence on an economy that refuses the logic of market ideology. That refusal is grounded in the conviction that the "other" in the economy is a neighbor. This God wills neighborliness and will accept no alternative.

Chapter 3

LIBERTY

JB: THE PROBLEM OF LIBERTY IS DOUBLE-SIDED. IN *Escape from Freedom*, Erich Fromm writes about two forms of liberty, "freedom from" and "freedom to." Each of these phrases grammatically implies a noun waiting at the end of the phrase, to complete the particular conceptualization of liberty. In the mainstream American ethos, we are preoccupied with freedom *from*. The implied noun is large institutions, which have the tendency to constrain individuals, their creativity, industriousness, and desires. As the framers of the American Constitution understood, the most important institution in this respect is government. Having fought a revolution against a repressive monarch, that generation understood better than most the risks of overbearing government. They also represented Enlightenment sensibilities

50

articulated by John Locke in his *Second Treatise*, which held that individuals matter. So various checks and balances were negotiated and built into our political institutions to limit the way particular elements of government function and to protect certain inalienable rights of individuals.

Those concerned with government overreach today have a point. In historical terms, this is about wanting government to serve the people, as Lincoln enunciated at Gettysburg, rather than vice versa. And this concern is not simply some antiquated resentment of an overbearing king. The genuinely positive and profound achievements of government notwithstanding, the frustration with our polity today is not really that hard to understand.

Max Weber recognized early on how the "iron cage" of bureaucracy was closing in. He lamented that it is

> horrible to think that the world could one day be filled with nothing but those little cogs, little men clinging to little jobs and striving toward bigger ones. . . . This passion for bureaucracy . . . is enough to drive one to despair. . . . That the world should know no men but these: it is in such an evolution that we are already caught up, and the great question is therefore not how we can promote and hasten it, but what can we oppose to this machinery in order to keep a portion of mankind free from this parceling-out of the soul, from this supreme mastery of the bureaucratic way of life. (Weber 1944, 127–28)

Whether it is tax policy, health care, or the military, even the most diligent, intrepid experts have a hard time grasping all the contours of such institutions. Normal

citizens encounter stupefying organizational complexities that cost time, energy, money, and in some real
sense, freedom. Sometimes it feels like the best years of
our lives are spent filling out forms for health insurance
claims or taxes. No doubt a lot of business owners and
managers feel oppressed by the government regulations
they have to navigate.

I recall a colleague once describing the committee
system in our academic institution as embodying "evolution without natural selection": new species emerge,
but none ever dies out. That seems a fitting metaphor for
much of government bureaucracy, too.

The last several decades of farm bills is a good example. Policymakers, both those who are well intentioned
and those who are not, have worked with advocates
of various special interests (e.g., agribusiness, farmers,
low-income families, unions, consumers) as well as
elected officials intent on delivering political returns to
their home districts or lobbyists. The result is one complicated bill after another. Regulations pile up, resulting
in a Rube Goldberg kind of mess, the totality of which
few understand.

The one predictable element in the evolving maze
of farm bills, however, is steady support for corporate
agribusiness. Large subsidies are routinely provided for
industrial farms to produce a small range of crops, especially corn, which is overproduced and used in ways that
contribute to the obesity epidemic (Stiglitz 2015). This
is especially ironic since efforts to combat food insecurity have been intermittent at best and took another blow
when the Supplemental Nutrition Assistance Program
(SNAP, commonly called food stamps) was reduced by

some $8 billion by way of the Agricultural Act of 2014 (Nixon 2014). Needless to say, there are no easy fixes, but the basic structure of government is certainly part of the problem.

If that is not enough, though, there is also the behavior of those in charge, as suggested above. Strong documentation indicates that every president since World War II up through George W. Bush has told multiple lies to the American people (Alterman 2004). Certainly, many observers regard Barack Obama as no exception (e.g., see Hersh 2015). More generally, government officials are sometimes corrupt. Tom DeLay (Republican congressman from Texas), William Jefferson (Democratic congressman from Louisiana), George Ryan (Republican governor of Illinois), and Rod Blagojevich (Democratic governor of Illinois) are just some of the better-known politicians who were implicated while in public office, illustrating that financial corruption is a bipartisan tradition maintained in different levels of government.

When leaders act up, whether it is lying, breaking laws, having extramarital sex in the Oval Office, or just pursuing misguided policies, citizens often feel unable to respond in any substantive way (see Sica 2015). We hear about government agencies spying on American citizens. Various legal efforts attempt to limit reproductive rights or dictate who can marry whom. Our political processes inordinately favor incumbents at all levels of government. Approval of the Congress is at an all-time low. All of these patterns contribute to cynicism, bitterness, and, understandably, the preoccupation with freedom *from*.

Similar issues of unfreedom unfold in other organizational contexts, namely through the sprawling influence of multinational corporations—influence that is much less evident in public discourse. Whereas no individual is "too big to fail," some companies can break a lot of rules and then get out of jail for free, as it were. Not only do some corporations have the rights of individuals—"Corporations are people, my friend," as presidential candidate Mitt Romney claimed—they have some privileges that transcend individual rights, such as the possibility of being bailed out when they have run out of money.

In most cases, individuals check their constitutional rights at the door when they sign a contract with a private employer. Think of religion, assembly, speech, or firearms, for example. Conversely, corporations can dictate policies related to a range of individual behaviors. Some companies legally influence their employees' medical choices, issues of sexuality, religious practices, and other decisions usually thought of as private. The Hobby Lobby case is a famous example. The retail arts and crafts chain successfully defended its right to not provide emergency contraceptive coverage through its employees' medical care. Wal-Mart, in another example, has restrictive policies against employees who are married dating other employees, even if they are separated from their spouses.

Such practices may not always be wrong. How can a private organization run if it is not allowed to actualize its values? And aren't owners and managers permitted to have a moral compass that shapes their work? Indeed, society is not possible if the group (whether it is a family, voting district, or company) cannot secure a degree of compliance from each individual member with certain dominant norms.

But how far should this freedom go? The key word here is *degree*. An obvious line of demarcation is that one person's freedom *to* cannot impose on another's freedom *from*, and vice versa. "Your liberty ends," the old adage goes, "where my nose begins" (see Shapiro 2006), or as one of my colleagues put it, "*you* can jump out of a plane, for all I care, just don't land on *me*."

There was a time when the average citizen could ignore the power of corporations. If you wanted to work for or buy from a large firm, no problem. If you didn't, also not a problem. You could buy goods from people you knew who could tell you what was in the products and how they were made. You could avoid billboards, turn off the TV or radio, and generally think about other things. You had that kind of freedom.

For the average citizen today, that is basically not possible. Corporations in the Fortune 500 account for some 16.3 percent of the private sector workforce and some 57 percent of all profits. More importantly, they are connected through similar biographical backgrounds and related families of owners and managers, overlapping boards of directors, policy-planning networks, shared economic and political interests, and active coordination (see Domhoff 2014).

The people and products associated with the corporate community are everywhere. The influence of such organizations on ideas, opinions, policy, and culture is in fact inescapable, and has been for several decades. In this context, is it possible we would not know if we were not free? "The greatest trick the Devil ever pulled was convincing the world he didn't exist," Kevin Spacey's character, Verbal, explains in *The Usual Suspects.*

And now there is a new factor in play. Before the Information Revolution, use of digital technology was first a rare luxury and then later a familiar privilege. Today it is a matter of basic functional dependency in all walks of life. The Pew Research Center reports that more than 80 percent of American adults now use computers (Fox and Rainie 2014). Across the land, it is increasingly hard to get medical care, complete school, land a job, secure legal advice, connect with your friends, or find out what time a movie starts without using digital technology. Of course it can be done (e.g., my coauthor daily makes a strong effort), but it has become relatively more difficult and comparatively disadvantageous to carry out all these basic tasks without the new technology.

According to one recent analysis, digital advertising in the United States accounted for $42.6 billion in revenue in 2013. A large bulk of that, $17.7 billion, was from digital display advertising. Five major technology companies—Facebook, Google, Yahoo, Microsoft, and AOL—accounted for more than half of that revenue (Olmstead 2014).

Yes, there is more information and in many cases greater efficiency. So what is the problem? The issue is how relentless, surround-sound—and surround-sight—advertising is built into the communication systems (Gitlin 2002; Kilbourne 1999). Much of the Internet cannot be accessed without subjecting oneself to the unfiltered claims of marketing. That might be arousing the roughly two-thirds of Americans who express support for more regulation of advertising. The use of personal information is another wrinkle here. Ninety-one percent of Americans either "agree" or "strongly agree" that "consumers have lost control over how personal information is collected and used by companies" (Madden 2014).

This perceived loss of consumers' control points to something even more fundamental. What the Internet is selling, above all, is an idealized version of our selves. The fragmented, superficial, high-speed qualities of communicating online appear to be literally changing our brains (Carr 2011). We have less capacity for disciplined consideration of complicated arguments or evidence. First, different companies stealthily gather tons of information about me. Then, whenever I search for something on the Internet, I am guided to information, products, and people already known to appeal to me. Beyond that cognitive corralling, though, I am taught that the real brand I should worry about is me. My status, my well-being, will be assessed in terms of "hits," "likes," "friends," and "followers." My concern for attention motivates me to become the marketed self.

The Internet is full of guidance about how I can get people to pay attention to me online. What is the ultimate goal? The perfect selfie. (Not a self-portrait, autobiography, reflection, or anything else that involves true self-examination.) A single moment—because virtual life is ephemeral. A deeply compelling context—I was there! The most important thing in the world, me, right in the middle—often a happy and childish but sexualized version of me. And a vast audience looking at me just as they adore the revered icons of our era, celebrities. The intentional packaging of the self in this way is a kind of quasi-commodification for which the return is not monetary profit but attention. (Well, at the very top, for the likes of Kim Kardashian, it is both, as demonstrated by her book of selfies entitled *Selfish*.) The performance of cheerfulness inures us to a life without tedium or complexity. And this self-inflicted objectification trivializes more genuine self-reflection. Not surprisingly, there is now a large research literature in psychology analyzing how narcissism is related to the new social media (i.e., to what extent does Twitter or Facebook attract or produce narcissists?).

All of this is good news for market-based fundamentalism (Marwick 2013). This kind of loyalty to oneself limits any complicating commitment to other principles or groups. The market is pleased to have such active consumers who fret a bit about how personal information is handled but mostly think about buying and selling, including ourselves. All of which raises a question, how free is the selfie-seeking self?

This conceptual colonization of Americans' consciousness socializes us to forget the ways we actually are free. Think of the most precious things in life that cost very little—quality time with loved ones, encounters with nature, meditation, or prayer—and the special value of those things that do not need marketing—like real art, fresh vegetables, homemade games, a really good conversation, clean water, exercise. To overlook the value of such freedom is a kind of captivity.

Some major cities have laws against "aggressive panhandling." A cup held by the outstretched hand of a poor person begging for a gift is unsightly and makes people uncomfortable. As a breach of personal space and a disruption to other intents, such a request might feel invasive. But this is hardly the most intrusive request most of us encounter on any given day. The integration of endless advertising into search engines, social media sites, and other communication hubs has an aggressive quality, too. Increasingly difficult to avoid, such demands for attention can only be ignored with firm resolve.

And it may be just the tip of the iceberg. A related question of freedom (*from* and *to*) is being vigorously debated right now over the issue of so-called net neutrality. How we get information about almost anything via the Internet—where we get it from, how fast we get it, and what other information we have to receive along with it—is all at stake. For each of us, the key factors in answering these questions will be determined by how much money we have and which communication companies we do business with, *if*—and this is a rather consequential if—the opponents of net neutrality have their way.

Net neutrality is the idea that anyone with access to the Internet is able to access all public sites in the same way, depending on individual carrying capacity. This is analogous to the way public roads work for American drivers. Anyone can go anywhere, depending on your car, fuel, and driving skill. You might have personal limitations, but the roads are open. Net neutrality is just like this sort of road neutrality. The alternative is the commodification of the Internet so your capacity to get any information is dependent on both your ability to pay service providers and with whom you choose to do business.

Anyone who helps build the infrastructure of the Internet, like, say Google, has a right to defray their costs and profit from their efforts. So goes the reasoning of those arguing against net neutrality. There is of course some logic to that argument. The same was said about toll roads in medieval Europe. And perhaps that is the point. The logic is medieval. It predates the rights of citizenship. It negates the modern consensus that we all have a common stake in protecting basic freedoms for one another.

For now, the key principle of net neutrality seems to be secure (McMillan 2014; 2015). The immediate threat is not differential access or speed, but rather the screening of information on the part of the big guys. There are already indications that some large providers will attempt to filter content that travels via the Internet in ways that serve their own moral priorities and profits. Verizon and AT&T have each tried to revise "Terms of Service" with customers to restrict any online communication that is damaging to their reputation or those of parent, subsidiaries, or affiliate companies. Comcast has tried to use filtering technology to block peer-to-peer networks who might want to carry out private transactions (e.g., sell videos to one another). Verizon cut off instant-messaging technology for the pro-abortion-rights group NARAL. The company stated that it would not provide service for any group "that seeks to promote an agenda or distribute content that, in its discretion, may be seen as controversial or unsavory to any of our users." For a time, Time Warner's AOL blocked all emails mentioning an advocacy group that opposed one of its policies. Talk about biased censorship!

In effect, there are questions of access, equality, and freedom all at stake in the debate about net neutrality (see Stanley 2010). We do not have to imagine what communication would be like if tyrants controlled the Internet. We need only look to what passes for mainstream political discourse to see how those with particular politics might treat others with polarized views.

In short, our epoch is dominated by the machinations of two colossal institutions, the state and the corporation, against which individuals and other kinds of institutions have little leverage. Even for affluent Americans, this circumstance can be morally claustrophobic. Some feel a panicky sense that the daily choices they make necessarily involve some painful combination of ethical compromise (lesser of two evils) or mind-numbing escapism. How many of us grapple with how our taxes are used to fund foreign wars or other policies we do not support, our inescapable use of fossil fuels, our reliance on poorly treated labor in this and (mostly) other countries, our compliance in an unsustainable food system, our dependence on digital technology saturated with manipulative advertising, or our ingestion of degrading popular culture?

And for Americans who live with material scarcity, the situation is even more pressing. Managing any kind of resistance to the powers that be—by way of political influence, legal recourse, relocation, quitting, vacation, therapy, activism, or other avenues that sometimes help—is that much more difficult for the poor.

However, this is just one kind of challenge related to not having freedom *from* powerful institutions. The more repressive sort of confinement for the poor relates to the other preposition, freedom *to* realize your life chances. Hence, the problem of freedom very much relates to the problem of care. Imagine not having the resources to provide your child with proper nutrition and health care. Almost fifty million Americans are food insecure. Sixteen million American children are poor. What would we say to the child who cannot stay awake in school because he never gets a full night's rest in a comfortable, safe bed and never eats breakfast? He is poor and unlucky. We might also say that he is not free—not free to cultivate and pursue his dreams. His rights have been alienated from him. The problem of liberty cuts in this direction, too.

What could be done? One recent study documents that the federal minimum wage in 2012 ($7.25) was worth 30 percent less than it was in 1968. In 2012, some 66 percent of minimum-wage workers were employed by large firms (those with at least one hundred employees). Among the fifty largest employers of low-wage workers, average compensation for top executives was $9.4 million (National Employment Law Project 2012).

A majority of economists now support some action on this front and believe it would help alleviate inequality (IGM Forum 2013). More than 70 percent of Americans in a recent poll agree (Scheiber and Sussman 2015). Thus the experts and people concur. The main argument against raising the minimum wage is that it would constrain job creation by raising the costs of production. (No doubt, most companies do not want to hire more people in any case. The so-called job creators hate creating jobs, again, because it raises production costs.) This argument only makes sense, however, in a universe where unlimited executive pay uncoupled from performance is taken as a given (see United States Department of Labor 2015). That is, the priority of enhancing pay or creating jobs for regular people loses out to maintaining exorbitant compensation for those at the top. The bonuses paid to Wall Street executives on top of their annual salaries mentioned above, some $28.5 million to about 167,800 employees, was double the aggregate pay of the roughly 1.3 million full-time federal minimum-wage workers (Anderson 2015). Corporate efforts to contain overhead costs should begin with such expensive and irrational practices.

The real reason for this moral stain is the collaboration of top executives and the boards of directors of private firms (Bogle 2005; Domhoff 2014). The public rationale is that this is what the market yields. To get the most able executives, they have to be paid at such a scale. Bonuses on the heels of declining profits, however, expose this lie—as does the success of corporations where such over-the-top pay and bonuses are not the norm.

Needless to say, raising wages past a certain level would be counterproductive. Nor would robust minimum-wage laws solve everything. Different societies have made different choices about how to provide for their members. Throughout American history, we have used minimum-wage laws, government assistance to the infirm, government assistance to the elderly, government assistance to the unemployed, government-guaranteed employment, collective bargaining rights, public education, philanthropy, charity, employer paternalism, informal communalism, and various other measures, which have at times been effective in protecting the material interests of U.S. citizens. But all of these ideas are basically under assault.

These patterns—including our threatened freedom from government influence and corporate control over digital resources and the carefully maintained material insecurity of many Americans—might make us wonder about authentic freedom. Together, they indicate that the risks of the problem of liberty are more expansive than current public discourse leads us to believe.

WB : THE TRANSITION IN ANCIENT ISRAEL FROM A tribal society to a monarchal system happened very quickly. King David became king in Israel by covenantal agreement with tribal elders: "So all the elders of Israel came to the king at Hebron; and King David made a covenant with them at Hebron before the LORD, and they anointed David king over Israel" (2 Sam. 5:3).

Israel's pedagogical and liturgical traditions worked hard to assert and assure that royal power was understood in covenantal ways that held the king responsible and that curbed royal power. Thus the Mosaic memory insisted that Israel's king must be "one from your community" who is familiar with covenantal requirements (Deut. 17:15). That embedment in covenant was designed to curb the usurpatious power of the throne: "He must not acquire many horses for himself. . . . And he must not acquire many wives for himself, or else his heart will turn away; also silver and gold he must not acquire in great quantity for himself" (vv. 16–17). The tradition recognized that the seduction of horses (arms), silver and gold (accumulated wealth), and wives (political alliances) would advance the singular power of the king at the expense of the covenantal community.

Even the liturgical recital in the Jerusalem temple affirmed a vision of the king as an advocate for justice for the poor that would keep royal policy in touch with socioeconomic reality:

> Give the king your justice, O God,
>   and your righteousness to a king's son.
> May he judge your people with righteousness,
>   and your poor with justice. . . .
> May he defend the cause of the poor of the people,
>   give deliverance to the needy,
>   and crush the oppressor. . . .
> For he delivers the needy when they call,
>   the poor and those who have no helper.
> He has pity on the weak and the needy,
>   and saves the lives of the needy.
>   (Ps. 72:1–2, 4, 12–13)

A king who is committed to the needy in society is not likely to move in a self-serving, absolutizing direction. Indeed, this liturgical psalm judges that long life and prosperity for the monarchy are deeply linked to social policy that attends to the vulnerable.

Given that background and ongoing advocacy, it is astonishing that we have no narrative of covenantal agreement whereby Solomon, David's son, became king. Instead of a negotiation for power and authority, we read only that Solomon came to royal power through a strong-arm coup (see W. Brueggemann 2005). Thus in rapid succession, in a narrative that anticipates *The*

Godfather, Solomon systematically and violently elimi-
nated all political opposition:

> Concerning his brother Adonijah, rival for the
> throne: "So King Solomon sent Benaiah son of
> Jehoiada; he struck him down, and he died" (1
> Kgs. 2:25).
> Concerning Joab, the strongest military leader:
> "Solomon sent Benaiah son of Jehoiada, saying,
> 'Go, strike him down.' . . . Then Benaiah son of
> Jehoiada went up and struck him down and killed
> him" (vv. 29, 34).
> Concerning Shimei, remnant of the northern Saul
> party: "Then the king commanded Benaiah son of
> Jehoiada; and he went out and struck him down,
> and he died" (v. 46).
> Concerning Abiathar, the priest who supported
> Adonijah: "So Solomon banished Abiathar from
> being priest to the LORD. . . . and the king put the
> priest Zadok in the place of Abiathar" (vv. 27, 35).

By force of arms, Solomon made himself an absolute
ruler.

We do not have in ancient Israel anything like a
corporation or a collage of corporations. But what we
do have is an absolute king who allowed no rivals, who
claimed all assets, and who was able to establish a totalism that paralleled the kind of totalism we now find in
our global economy. Indeed, Solomon, in his known
world, was a practitioner of globalization, for he was at
the center of international commerce.

The analog between *ancient Solomon* and *contemporary*

corporate totalism is compelling enough if we attend to the "totality" that Emmanuel Levinas has sketched out (Levinas 1969). That totality intends to establish an all-comprehensive, socioeconomic, political system that allows nothing outside its domain. It occupies the imagination of the community in a way that precludes imagining any alternatives because of the force, the seduction, and the attractiveness of the system. Robert Lifton, moreover, has traced the way in which such totality characteristically moves to absolutism and finally to violence that silences all alternatives (Lifton 2011, 67–68, 381).

While we have, in much church teaching, a soft, romantic impression of Solomon as the "wise king" and temple builder, the text itself suggests that such notions concerning Solomon are rather the decor of propaganda that seeks to conceal the tough and uncompromising monopoly that he was able to establish. As a result, a study of Solomon permits an interesting and illuminating analog between that ancient, self-serving regime and the narrative, variously constructed in our society, concerning the collusion of governmental power and corporate wealth outside of which nothing is imaginable. For good reason, Enrique Dussel has added to the notion of "globalization" the counterterm of "exclusion" (Dussel 2013). Thus his subtitle is, "In the Age of Globalization and Exclusion."

This is an exact characterization of Solomon's regime that had a global reach but excluded from consideration any voice other than the ones he had co-opted. So in our time globalization (and its tool of implementation, "development") has created a make-believe world of vast wealth at the expense of peasant labor. It is for good reason that Solomon can be reckoned in ancient Israel as the one who brought Pharaoh's assumptions and practices to effect within Israel. It cannot be unimportant that Solomon was the son-in-law of a pharaoh (1 Kgs. 3:1; 7:8; 9:24; 11:1).

We may identify five facets of Solomon's totalism that have a ring of contemporaneity:

1. This totalism has an economic base. This was achieved through a carefully developed tax collection agency that extracted revenue from peasants for the royal treasury. First Kings 4:7–20 details the tax arrangements: "Solomon had twelve officials over all Israel, who provided food for the king and his household; each one had to make provision for one month in the year" (v. 7).

It is worth noting that two of his sons-in-law, Benabinadab and Ahimaaz, presided over tax districts; it must have been a thriving business sustained in part by nepotism (vv. 11, 15). The revenue from taxation was supplemented by cheap labor practices, termed in the text, "forced labor." In 1 Kings 9:22 it is asserted that cheap labor (slavery) did not extend to Solomon's Israelite compatriots: "But of the Israelites Solomon made no slaves; they were the soldiers, they were his officials, his commanders, his captains, and the commanders of his chariotry and cavalry."

But 5:13–16, to the contrary, suggests that Israelites were included in the program. Indeed, Solomon had a cabinet officer designated as in charge of forced labor, which I suppose we would name as "secretary of labor": "King Solomon was king over all Israel; and these were his high officials. . . . Adoniram son of Abda was in charge of the forced labor" (4:1, 6).

Along with taxation and cheap labor, Solomon's regime is reported to have been a shrewd and dominant force in the international economy:

> Solomon gathered together chariots and horses; he had fourteen hundred chariots and twelve thousand horses, which he stationed in the chariot cities and with the king in Jerusalem. . . . Solomon's import of horses was from Egypt and Kue, and the king's traders received them from Kue at a price. A chariot could be imported from Egypt for six hundred shekels of silver, and a horse for one hundred fifty; so through the king's traders they were exported to all the kings of the Hittites and the kings of Aram. (10:26, 28–29)

He was an arms dealer!

Along with armaments, his regime was at the center of international trade:

> For the king had a fleet of ships of Tarshish at sea with the fleet of Hiram. Once every three years the fleet of ships of Tarshish used to come bringing gold, silver, ivory, apes, and peacocks.
>
> Thus King Solomon excelled all the kings of the earth in riches and in wisdom. The whole earth sought the presence of Solomon to hear his wisdom, which God had put into his mind. Every one of them brought a present, objects of silver and gold, garments, weaponry, spices, horses, and mules, so much year by year. (10:22–25)

That inventory of wealth was given specificity by the narrative of the "summit meeting" of Solomon with the Queen of Sheba that was to assure commercial arrangements (1 Kgs. 10:1–10). Thus the combination of taxation, cheap labor, and trade made Solomon's regime, as it is remembered in the tradition, an immense force that carried everything before it. The leverage that it could assert included both the domestic economy and the global economy, which was dominated, so we are told, by Jerusalem.

2. Given these practices and policies, it is not a surprise that Solomon's mode of operation was one of endless confiscation of everything that it could touch or reach. The wealth of the regime was beyond imagination:

> The weight of *gold* that came to Solomon in one year was six hundred sixty-six talents of *gold*, besides that which came from the traders and from the business of the merchants, and from all the kings of Arabia and the governors of the land. King Solomon made two hundred large shields of beaten *gold*; six hundred shekels of *gold* went into each large shield. He made three hundred shields of beaten *gold*; three minas of *gold* went into each shield; and the king put them in the House of the Forest of Lebanon. The king also made a great ivory throne, and overlaid it with the finest *gold*. . . . Nothing like it was ever made in any kingdom. (10:14–18, 20)

Along with the confiscation of all of the wealth of his domain, he exhibited himself as a patron of the arts:

> God gave Solomon very great wisdom, discernment, and breadth of understanding as vast as the sand on the seashore, so that Solomon's wisdom surpassed the wisdom of all the people of the east, and all the wisdom of Egypt. . . . He composed three thousand proverbs, and his songs numbered a thousand and

five. He would speak of trees, from the cedar that is in the Lebanon to the hyssop that grows in the wall; he would speak of animals, and birds, and reptiles, and fish. People came from all the nations to hear the wisdom of Solomon; they came from all the kings of the earth who had heard of his wisdom. (4:29–30, 31–34)

While we do not know, given what we have already seen, we can conclude that his collection (production) of songs and proverbs was not unlike a wealthy person who collects art without having an interest in art as anything but a valuable commodity. The classification of all the species in verse 33 suggests an attempt to organize (and so control?) all available knowledge in an encyclopedic manner, with "all knowledge" to match "all wealth" and "all power."

His avarice had no limits. As a result, his narrative ends in 1 Kings 11:3 with a report on his "collection" of women: "Among his wives were seven hundred princesses and three hundred concubines."

It is not likely that the numbers suggest a focus on sexuality. Rather, they probably reflect political alliances whereby Solomon constructed a network of power relationships cemented by marriages. But of course one cannot separate such political power from the need to exhibit virility. The practice of such "collecting" indicates that the regime had no limit in its capacity for accumulation.

3. Every hegemonic regime finally does not depend upon force, but upon the control of the media so that public imagination is monopolized. In the ancient world, the temple—managed and sponsored by royal authority—was the media center of society. So it was for

Solomon. The temple must have dominated imagination the way the imaginative force of ESPN or the NFL dominate the life of our culture. The text details the construction of the temple (1 Kgs. 6–7). The accent is on the artistic detail of the temple that served to exhibit the enormous wealth of the regime, which is readily interpreted as God's blessing and approval. The story of the temple as a show of opulence is dominated by the seemingly endless inventory of gold, the visible measure of success and domination:

> The interior of the inner sanctuary was twenty cubits long, twenty cubits wide, and twenty cubits high; he overlaid it with pure *gold*. He also overlaid the altar with cedar. Solomon overlaid the inside of the house with pure *gold*, then he drew chains of *gold* across, in front of the inner sanctuary, and overlaid it with *gold*. Next he overlaid the whole house with *gold*, in order that the whole house might be perfect; even the whole altar that belonged to the inner sanctuary he overlaid with *gold*. (6:20–22)

> So Solomon made all the vessels that were in the house of the LORD; the *golden* altar, the *golden* table for the bread of the Presence, the lampstands of pure *gold*, five on the south side and five on the north, in front of the inner sanctuary; the flowers, the lamps, and the tongs, of *gold;* the cups, snuffers, basins, dishes for incense, and firepans, of pure *gold*; the sockets for the doors of the innermost part of the house, the most holy place, and for the doors for the nave of the temple, of *gold*.
> Thus all the work that King Solomon did on the house of the LORD was finished. Solomon brought in the things that his father David had dedicated, the silver, the *gold*, and the vessels, and stored them in the treasuries of the house of the LORD. (7:48–51)

This account of opulent construction is matched in 8:1–16 by the dramatic and showy dedication of the temple. The occasion must have been as dramatic and showy as the halftime show at the Super Bowl. The accent is on extravagance, which is marked by the wholesale sacrifice of "many sheep and oxen" in an exhibit of over-the-top piety. The real purpose of the drama, however, is to assert the unqualified (absolute) divine authorization of the regime. This includes the choral anthem (vv. 12–13); the "blessing" uttered by the king, not unlike a presidential "God bless America" (vv. 14–21); and the assertion of durable divine commitment to the dynasty (vv. 22–26).

It is credible to think that such a show of piety, wealth, and extravagance, all performed with divine approval, must have made certain that the authority of the regime was placed beyond doubt or question. The temple was an awesome artistic project, so that life in the world would be viewed through the lens of this highly compelling work of art.

4. The achievement of such an economic-political-artistic monopoly would not have been the work of a single actor, not even Solomon. Thus we may imagine that Solomon is surrounded and supported by a host of admirers and advocates who benefited from the enterprise. Thus the enterprise required and recruited a corps of devotees who are rightly reckoned as an elite who shared in and profited from the monopoly. In 4:22 we have a report on one day's food provision for the royal court: "Solomon's provision for one day was thirty cors of choice flour, and sixty cors of meal, ten fat oxen, and twenty pasture-fed cattle, one hundred sheep, besides

deer, gazelles, roebucks, and fatted fowl." One is struck by the extravagance that must have fed a large body of royal operatives. More than that, it is a diet dominated by meat, no doubt amid a peasant economy in which meat was rarely on offer.

In 10:8, moreover, the Queen of Sheba exclaims about Solomon's prosperity and wisdom: "Happy are your wives! Happy are these your servants, who continually attend you and hear your wisdom!" The double affirmation of verse 8 concerns "your wives" and "your servants." In the Hebrew text the term here rendered as "wives" is "men," which would be a parallel to "your servants." We may take the two terms together to mean "your royal entourage," who enjoyed the surplus wealth that the combination of taxation, cheap labor, and trade made possible.

Thus the practice of economic extravagance, media monopoly, and a privileged elite amount to a domination that is a compelling parallel to our own current social context of taxation of the middle class, global trade, and cheap labor. The combination yields a privileged elite who strut in celebrity and security. Solomon's enterprise is the process of making some rich at the expenses of many others. This enterprise is a singular embodiment of that process. For good reason Almeida Garrett can aver: "I ask the political economists and the moralists if they have ever calculated the number of individuals who must be condemned to misery, overwork, demoralization, degradation, rank ignorance, overwhelming misfortune and utter penury in order to produce one rich man" (from *Viagens Na Minha Terra* [*Travels in My Land*], as quoted in Saramago 2012, frontispiece).

Solomon is that rich man! He is, moreover, surrounded by others he has made rich. By the end, Solomon's success of the old authorization of Moses (Deut.
17:14–20) and the old liturgical affirmation (Ps.
72) are no more than a memory that has been effectively
defeated by the power of "more."

5. Such a regime, we could imagine, would last to
perpetuity. Surely its beneficiaries must have imagined
so. It is something of a jolt to recognize in the narrative
itself the seeds of its undoing, which came quickly. We
may identify three expressions of disjunction by which
the imagined totalism of Solomon turned out to be
unsustainable.

a. The imagined absolutism of the regime is
challenged in the narrative by the conditionality
of "if" that asserts the requirements of the God
who had become the patron of the regime (W.
Brueggemann 2005, 139–59).

> *If* you will walk in my ways, keeping my
> statutes and my commandments, as your
> father David walked, *then* I will lengthen
> your life. (3:14)
>
> *If* you will walk in my statutes, obey my ordi-
> nances, and keep all my commandments
> by walking in them, *then* I will establish my
> promise with you, which I made to your
> father David. (6:12)
>
> *If* you will walk before me, as David your
> father walked, with integrity of heart and
> uprightness, doing according to all that
> I have commanded you, and keeping my

statutes and my ordinances, *then* I will establish your royal throne over Israel for-ever, as I promised to your father David, saying, "There shall not fail you a succes-sor on the throne of Israel." (9:4–5)

The divine "if," implied in Psalm 72, appeals to the old covenant tradition voiced already in Exodus 19:5. In that tradition the maintenance of the regime depends upon honoring Torah commandments. Thus the regime is early put on notice. The utterance of the "if" is modest and understated in the narrative. But the condition-ality is relentless and uncompromising. In the end it could not be defeated or overcome, even by such a monopoly.

b. In the concluding narrative of 1 Kings 11:29–39 the prophet Ahijah meets Solomon's secretary of labor. He whispers in his ear the outrageous claim that the divine endorsement of Solomon has been withdrawn: "See, I am about to tear the kingdom from the hand of Solomon, and will give you ten tribes" (11:31).

Such an uncredentialed threat, given as divine resolve, is of little import in the face of a well-established regime. Except that is how trou-ble begins: when someone begins to notice and to utter out loud the jeopardy in which the regime stands. Totalizing regimes are enormously vigi-lant about such uncredentialed possibilities that fall outside the domain of managed imagination. For that reason, Solomon took vigorous steps:

"Solomon sought therefore to kill Jeroboam, but Jeroboam promptly fled to Egypt, to King Shishak of Egypt, and remained in Egypt until the death of Solomon" (11:40).

His steps, however, were steps that did not succeed. Now the word of jeopardy is set loose in the world, the utterance of such a possibility of demise that brings the "if" of divine condition to concrete political reality. It is a possibility that the regime wanted to keep unimagined. The undoing of Solomon has been set loose in society, a truth that could not be contained within the totalizing apparatus he had set in place.

c. But the subtle "if" of divine condition and the wild utterance of the uncredentialed by themselves constitute no sustainable threat. What finally matters is the moment when subterranean threats take on mass movement, such as in 1 Kings 12, which is nothing less than a tax revolt. That revolt does not happen until after the death of Solomon. But the seeds of demise are already there. The peasant population, weary of tax burdens that support royal extravagance, seized the moment of the new king, Solomon's son Rehoboam, to assert its peasant power and to resist the tax burden imposed by the Jerusalem elite. Rehoboam, schooled in royal privilege and entitlement, refused, clearly underestimating the resistance of the 99 percent in ancient Israel. The outcome of the royal refusal was resistance and finally rebellion that caused the collapse of Solomon's united monarchy:

> When King Rehoboam sent Adoram, who was task-
> master over the forced labor, all Israel stoned him
> to death King Rehoboam then hurriedly mounted
> his chariot to flee to Jerusalem. So Israel has been
> in rebellion against the house of David to this day.
> (12:18–19)

We cannot trace the connection between *the uncredentialed utterance of Ahijah* and *the mass uprising* in Israel,
but the narrator finds in the two acts taken together
the work of YHWH, who finally will destabilize the
regime of Solomon: "So the king did not listen to the
people, because it was a turn of affairs brought about
by the LORD that he might fulfill his word, which the
LORD had spoken by Ahijah the Shilonite to Jeroboam
son of Nebat" (12:15). The narrator dares to say that
it was none other than YHWH, the ultimate authority that Solomon had reduced to a patron, who finally
broke the totalism and ended the illusion of Solomon's
extravagant social experiment in his self-indulgence and
self-sufficiency.

The narrator cannot be sure, but seems to suspect
that something hidden and inscrutable is going on in
public history that the hegemony of Solomon cannot
outflank. It is the attestation of the narrative that even
the absolutism of Solomon is quite penultimate and
must yield to the ultimacy of YHWH. It is of immense
importance that this allusion to YHWH's hidden governance is embedded in a narrative of tax revolt, suggesting a convergence or collusion between *the will of God*
and *the action of the 99 percent.* The connection is elusive,
but the narrator will allow for it.

The Solomonic crisis, a crisis of self-indulgent extravagance and inexplicable collapse, is belatedly summarized by Jeremiah. Jeremiah is from the hometown of Abiathar, the priest exiled by Solomon (see Jer. 1:1; 11:21). We may, beyond that geographic locus, imagine that Jeremiah was schooled in the anti-Solomonic conviction of Abiathar, even though he came many generations later. Perhaps he had imagined exactly the failed nature of Solomon's "corporate hegemony" when he voiced the deep either-or of covenantal faith:

> Do not let the wise boast in their wisdom, do not let the mighty boast in their might, do not let the wealthy boast in their wealth; but let those who boast boast in this, that they understand and know me, that I am the LORD; I act with steadfast love, justice, and righteousness in the earth, for in these things I delight, says the LORD. (Jer. 9:23–24)

Chapter 4

LOYALTY

$\mathbf{JB}$: AMERICANS ARE AS BUSY AS EVER. BUT WE DO A LOT of things alone, as Robert Putnam documented more than a decade ago in his bestseller, *Bowling Alone.* This loss of durable relationships is evident throughout many parts of society but is especially pronounced in the private sector. "On average, U.S. corporations now lose half their customers in five years, half their employees in four, and half their investors in less than one," Frederick Reichheld declares. "We seem to face a future in which the only business relationships will be opportunistic transactions between virtual strangers" (Reichheld 2001, 1).

Given how much time we all spend at work and how influential corporations are in shaping the culture of other organizations and social life in general, this fluid quality has implications that reach far beyond job satisfaction and the bottom line. Collectively, we seem increasingly comfortable with disposability. From planned obsolescence, walk-in closets full of unused clothes, colossal landfills, the "status update" compulsion, Twitter, Tinder, and the other ephemeral connections we have to the world, there is something so wasteful and small-minded about it all.

The problem of loyalty is how people stick together. This was the main question that guided the lifelong inquiry of the eminent sociologist Émile Durkheim that started with his doctoral dissertation, *The Division of Labor in Society*. It is not just how government provides order and cultivates compliance, though that surely matters for the well-being of a modern society. More broadly, it is about how any group holds together. Even more fundamentally, it is about the concept of a group. It is about some deep sense of us. It is ultimately about love. The ideal of loyalty presumes a social context in which such taken-for-granted devotion is meaningful.

This question of loyalty has been a problem in America since before the Revolution. In some sense, the United States was founded on disloyalty. Religious dissidents sought independence from dominant religious and political bodies. Upon arrival in the new land, though, religious authorities had no easy time maintaining order as new disagreements kept popping up. Various religious movements in the early decades of the Massachusetts Bay Colony persistently sought more autonomy from those in charge (see Erikson 1966). Later, even as the colonists were united in their opposition to King George IV, General George Washington had a hard time securing the resources necessary to wage the military campaign against the British. They knew what they were against, as in many revolutions, but were less clear about what they were for (Ellis 2005).

Since then, local and regional ties in settings as diverse as Idaho, Maine, South Carolina, or Texas, have often seemed stronger than any loyalty to the federal government or the nation per se. Various tensions have at times divided Americans from one another. The Civil War continues to reverberate through electoral politics, as does the civil rights movement. The 1960s in general and the Vietnam War in particular are linked to unresolved questions about what the most important American values are. These and other historical events contribute to a complicated and contested sense of what it means to be American. For many citizens, political affiliation is now the most potent source of identity. "Being a Democrat or a Republican," David Brooks suggests, "becomes their ethnicity" (2016).

Related to such historical complexities, at least in modern society, is a dilemma social scientists call the "free rider problem." Individuals have a rational incentive to gain the collective goods (e.g., a viable ecosystem, military security, health care) available from their surrounding groups without paying the full cost of individual membership (e.g., sustainable consumption, taxes, lawfulness, cooperation). In the context of modern society where neither blood, land, nor creed provides a fixed foundation for social solidarity, this contradiction has intensified.

Durkheim hoped modern individuals would stick together on the basis of a shared sense of interdependence.

So much diversity in who we are, what we think, and what we do would motivate us to rely on one another. As important as the family was to moral education, in Durkheim's view, it was too varied and particular to serve this function for society as a whole. The main alternative for such socialization would be occupational and professional organizations, he suggested (Lukes 1973, 185).

This aspiration, however, proved to be wishful thinking. The primacy of the individual derived from the Protestant Reformation, the Age of Enlightenment, and the American Revolution, and thereby woven into the fabric of American history, has been augmented through active and strategic efforts of social elites (Madrick 2011). The most glaring examples leap out from the pages of our history during the Gilded Age, the Roaring Twenties, and the Reagan Revolution.

This is not to suggest that all individualism is bad, of course, or that these eras did not produce some good things. Moreover, the traditions of American individualism were historically complemented by shared values and civic concerns (Tocqueville 1970, vol. 2; Fukuyama 1996). Adam Smith is known for the individualism extolled in *The Wealth of Nations*. However, we too often forget his earlier masterpiece, *The Theory of Moral Sentiments*, in which he argues for the capacity and importance of human sympathy and compassion as well.

Still, sometimes the value of our common life and how it needs to be balanced with individual freedoms become shrouded, as it has at certain historical moments. How will our current moment be remembered in this regard? Managerial and professional elites today are a diverse group. In *The Revolt of the Elites and the Betrayal of*

Democracy, Christopher Lasch describes this "new class." They include "brokers, bankers, real estate promoters and developers, engineers, consultants of all kinds, systems analysts, scientists, doctors, publicists, publishers, editors, advertising executives, art directors, moviemakers, entertainers, journalists, television producers and directors, artists, writers, university professors" (1995, 34). Diverse yes, but similar in both material status and cultural lifestyle. Their class situation is a matter of trafficking in symbolic material, abstractions, images, and information.

"They send their children to private schools, insure themselves against medical emergencies, . . . and hire private security guards to protect themselves against the mounting violence against them. In effect, they have removed themselves from the common life," Lasch continues (1995, 45). "They gladly pay for private and suburban schools, private police, and private systems of garbage collection; but they have managed to relieve themselves, to a remarkable extent, of the obligation to contribute to the national treasury. Their acknowledgment of civic obligations does not extend beyond their own immediate neighborhoods" (47; see also R. Frank 2007).

As consequential as such personal choices are, elite selfishness has more destructive implications on the organizational level. Certain industries such as fast food, soda, tobacco, firearms, and alcohol knowingly peddle dangerous products that do damage to our collective well-being. Our special standing in the global community as a leader in obesity, homicide, and drunk driving is not compelling enough to rein in the practices of such businesses. Indeed, efforts to encourage such action have been met harshly and decisively. Just ask Oprah Winfrey, who had to spend over $1 million in legal fees defending herself against a lawsuit filed by Texas cattlemen when she complained about illegal and unhealthy meat production processes related to mad cow disease (see Nestle 2002).

Whether it is resisting taxation that would fund infrastructure or education among other public goods, seeking inexpensive labor elsewhere, or relying on government welfare programs to support underpaid employees, some corporations demonstrate little concern for the communities in which they do business (see Buchheit 2013). One study of 288 corporations found that between 2008 and 2012 they paid, on average, an effective federal income tax rate of 19.4 percent (well below the statutory 35 percent tax rate). More to the point, a third of them paid an effective tax rate of less than 10 percent during those years, and 39 percent paid nothing in federal income taxes, or even received refunds, in at least one of those years (McIntyre, Gardner, and Phillips 2014). Tax avoidance costs the United States upwards of $3 trillion a year, one estimate suggests, most of it benefiting the wealthiest (Buchheit 2015).

There is nothing wrong with earning money as long as other important principles are not completely negated. In any viable society, natural and human resources have to be at the center of such principles. There are certainly exceptional firms, like Mattel or Johnson & Johnson, known for their civic ideals. They are part of a rich tradition of corporate social responsibility in the United States. We have recently seen significant impact on

the part of certain businesses who have influenced gay
rights, removal of the Confederate battle flag, the interests of immigrants, and sustainability efforts (see Bruni
2015). Doing the right thing can be viable (see Capaldi
2005; Aguinis and Glavas 2012). But that tradition is
contrasted with another pattern of ruthlessness and the
"tyranny of the bottom line" (Bellah 1999). Whether it
is the vitality of unions, income distribution, wage rates,
employee benefits, employee relations writ large, tax
policy, ecological sustainability, institutional transparency, inclusive governance, or economic development,
there is plenty of evidence to suggest the latter tradition
has significant momentum.

"Loyalty to the country always," said Mark Twain.
"Loyalty to the government when it deserves it." But
the extreme cases, such as Monsanto, McDonald's, or
Glock, demonstrate the lack of loyalty toward the country or anyone else. Monsanto has somehow evaded
antitrust laws, crushed competitors, engaged in dubious advertising, and suppressed efforts to bring more
transparency to its practices. The effects of the "food"
sold by McDonald's on Americans' health are well
documented. Glock is a leader in the firearms industry,
which has orchestrated singular legal protections from
any liability associated with its products; its industry has
also been remarkably effective in suppressing systematic
research on the implications of the use of its products in
American society. Ugly, but surely not representative of
corporate America in general.

A more subtle and perhaps important problem is
hidden in plain sight. What is most successfully sold
by American corporations is the idea that everything is

and should be for sale. Everyone has a price. Everyone for him- or herself (see Kuttner 1999; Madrick 2011). "Brand loyalty" is in reality loyalty to no one. The average American first-grader has been exposed to thirty thousand advertisements, according to one estimate, and can identify two hundred brands (Schor 2004). This is not accidental because they happen to be nearby as their parents choose to get information about different products. It is because corporations hire scientists, artists, and lawyers to study how to reach children, and then actively target them. In every supermarket there is a shrine to cynicism and manipulation—it is the row of sugary breakfast cereals parents try to negotiate without being nagged by their children, children who have been won over through elaborate multimedia product placement and marketing. *Caveat emptor*, indeed.

There is a new kind of firm that works hard to cultivate the loyalty of its customers in novel ways. Some of them are vast megabrands like Disney and Marvel, which sell intertwined complexes of products and try to make consumers loyal to all of them and any of them.

But loyalty is an ideal that many corporations attempt to sell but increasingly do not embody in their own practices. The idea that a company would cultivate employees, grow their skills and craft, develop reciprocal relationships of mutual well-being, and over time earn employees' loyalty is becoming obsolete (see Sennett 2006; Uchitelle 2006).

Likewise, without the proper tax breaks, let alone sufficient profits, some corporations demonstrate scarce loyalty to consumers, local communities, or even American interests, for that matter. You would be hard-pressed to find any significant enterprise that has not demanded various tax breaks before they would set up shop. Not because it is right, but because they can. And not without consequence for all of us. For instance, Bloomberg estimates that tax exemptions on major sports stadiums cost the U.S. Treasury some $146 million a year (Kuriloff and Preston 2012). Loyalty is asked for but not given. Perhaps they do not feel government deserves loyalty at this time, as per Twain's wisdom. However, while various corporate leaders seek to dodge taxation and shrink the role of government, the foundation of our society is literally crumbling. The American Society of Civil Engineers has given our current national infrastructure a grade of D. That reflects inadequate management of roads, dams, bridges, ports, and waste, among other problems (American Society of Civil Engineers 2013).

Another kind of example was witnessed in the Great Recession of 2008. This was a national crisis during which Americans up and down the socioeconomic status ladder suffered severe losses. Between 2007 and 2009, average American family income declined by 17.4 percent (Saez 2015). The cost for our country was extensive on multiple fronts. According to one report (Irons 2009), this included long-term setbacks in education, economic opportunity, private investment, and entrepreneurial activity, and all the indirect implications of those problems.

Whereas the recession was inclusive, the recovery was not. During the first three years of the recovery, from 2009 to 2012, the top 1 percent of incomes increased by 34.7 percent, netting 91 percent of the aggregate income gains. The bottom 99 percent regained only 0.8 percent (Saez 2015).

The causes of the recession are complicated. No doubt, though, some executives lied and many were at least complicit in the deregulation movement that helped create the destructive conditions (see Posner 2009; Lewis 2010; Stiglitz 2015). To add insult to injury, not one CEO has been prosecuted (Irwin 2013). The galling insult is no accountability. The real injury, though, is a structural arrangement in which a small number of people can take huge risks with other people's lifework and then profit in any case. Ever see the movie *Trading Places?* "Tell him the good part," urges Mortimer Duke. "The good part," his brother Randolph responds, "is that, no matter whether our clients make money or lose money, Duke & Duke get the commissions." In real life, though, there is no sweet revenge at the end of the story.

Perhaps the worst implication of such self-interested maneuvering is that regular people are constantly offered the lesson that this is normal, the way to get ahead. Political leaders, economic elites, and iconic celebrities all model this behavior and encourage the same. As a result, looking out for Number One, skirting the rules, and getting away with it is rapidly becoming our national pastime. The irony here is that withholding generosity harms not only those denied the gift but also those who might have given. "The highest level of Maslow's hierarchy of needs, self-actualization," David Brooks (2016) notes, "is actually connected to the lowest level, group survival. People experience their highest joy in helping their neighbors make it through the day." In the absence of moral sensibilities that mediate greed, responsible governance necessitates structural arrangements that inhibit such narrow self-interest. Without such cultural or institutional arrangements, the problem of loyalty will remain unresolved.

WB: THE BOOKS OF 1 AND 2 KINGS (FROM WHICH we drew our portrayal of Solomon) trace in forty-seven chapters the monarchy in Israel over four hundred years concerning both the kings of northern Israel and the Davidic dynasty in Jerusalem. The account moves from the extravagant success of Solomon (1 Kgs. 3–11) to the sorry failure and demise of the dynasty of David (2 Kgs. 24–25). For the most part the account on offer is a royal chronicle that provides stereotypical prose concerning the succession of kings, their wars, and their temple reforms. The impression of the whole is an ordered, well-defined, and well-managed summary of official public history.

Something very strange and unexpected, however, happens in the midst of this highly disciplined and repetitious prose report. In the chapters that stretch from 1 Kings 17 through 2 Kings 9 (and later including 2 Kgs. 13:14–21), fifteen chapters in all, the prose recital of royal data is interrupted by a very different kind of narrative (W. Brueggemann 2001). The contrast in literary expression and genre is striking, suggesting that in these chapters we are in a very different epistemological milieu. That sharp difference in style and genre is commensurate with a dramatic change in content. Now instead of a chronicle of kings, we get narratives of prophetic characters, Elijah and Elisha. While dramatic attention in the narrative is drawn to Elijah and Elisha, other prophets also appear in this material. (In 1 Kgs. 20 there is a nameless prophet, and in chap. 22 Micaiah ben Imlah is featured.) The intrusion of these two "men of God" into the royal recital is abrupt and inexplicable.

The interruption begins with this dramatic assertion in 1 Kings 17:1:

> Now Elijah the Tishbite, of Tishbe in Gilead, said to Ahab, "As the LORD the God of Israel lives, before whom I stand, there shall be neither dew nor rain these years, except by my word."

We know nothing about Elijah except that he came from Gilead, a territory east of the Jordan at the far reach of royal control. All we know, and likely all that King Ahab knew, is that he is uncredentialed and without pedigree. But he utters! He breaks the royal recital with speech. He has direct access to the king and he claims immense authority, enough to command the rain clouds. Before he finishes the paragraph, we are told that he is directed by "the word of YHWH" that dispatches him amid the drought to which the king has no effective response. He is, from the outset, laden with power that lies beyond royal administration. In these few terse verses, this character is enunciated who will initiate a counterforce into the life of Israel, the force of prophetic, transformative power.

Before he finishes, Elijah will conduct two major dramatic scenes in the life of the king. In chapter 18 he will be the champion of YHWH, the God of the exodus narrative, who contests the authority of Baal, the god of agricultural fertility who has royal support in northern Israel. In chapter 21 he will contest royal notions of land confiscation by championing the old tribal notion of land as the inalienable inheritance of tribe and family. These two great public acts are enough to earn for Elijah the dismissive verdict from Ahab, his great adversary, that he is "my enemy" (21:20) and "troubler of Israel" (18:17), that is, disturber of royal control. The literary disruption of the royal chronicle is commensurate with the sociopolitical disruption caused by the prophet and the theological disruption caused by his championing of YHWH in the face of what he regards as shameless religious compromise by the royal household.

But our theme here is localism. For that we consider especially the narrative episodes in 1 Kings 17. In verses 8–16 Elijah comes upon a widow in Sidon; she represents, in the rhetoric of Israel, the socially and economically vulnerable who have been squeezed out of a viable life and who lack resources and protection. She dwells in an economy of scarcity: "As the Lord your God lives, I have nothing baked, only a handful of meal in a jar, and a little oil in a jug. I am now gathering a couple of sticks, so that I may go home and prepare it for myself and my son, that we may eat it, and die" (v. 12).

Elijah responds to her with fearless authority: "Do not be afraid" (v. 13). And then inexplicably, he transforms her scarcity into overflowing abundance: "'For thus says the Lord the God of Israel: The jar of meal will not be emptied and the jug of oil will not fail until the day that the Lord sends rain on the earth.' . . . The jar of meal was not emptied, neither did the jug of oil fail, according to the word of the Lord that he spoke by Elijah" (vv. 14, 16). We are not told how that happened. No explanation is offered and no curiosity is expressed.

The credit is only given to "the word of the LORD," a hovering transformative power that lies beyond the administration of the king.

In a second episode that follows immediately, by a more complex narrative route, Elijah gives life back to the son of the widow: "Your son is alive" (v. 23).

These two narratives attest that a power for life is loosed in the society of Israel. That power, moreover, is carried by this uncredentialed character who is willing and able to enter into the desperate life of peasant people. The entire action takes place outside the zone of royal administration, so that what we have is an alternative reading of social reality that disregards and, by implication, defies the authority of the crown. The locus of Elijah's work in these two narratives is in the local community in which neighborly possibility is restored. Because these two narratives in 17:8–16 and 17–24 precede the great public events of chapters 18 and 21, we can conclude that all of these events are the work of neighborly activity outside the reach of official power arrangements. Real power for life lies outside of the official economy of authorized governance.

Our theme becomes more poignant in the work of Elisha, who is Elijah's heir and successor (see 19:19–21). We know nothing of him either. He is a peasant farmer found "plowing," without credential or pedigree. While he is not reckoned in the tradition to have been as formidable as his predecessor Elijah, by the time he finishes he will have caused an even greater disruption in the literary memory of Israel, for he is featured in a much larger collection of narratives.

He begins his transformative work at the death of

Elijah (2 Kgs. 2:1–12). He claims the authority of Elijah by dramatically taking the "mantle" of Elijah as a
sign of empowerment and authority. Immediately upon
receipt of the mantle, it is reported: "He took the mantle
of Elijah that had fallen from him, and struck the water,
saying, 'Where is the LORD, the God of Elijah?' When
he had struck the water, the water was parted to the one
side and to the other, and Elisha went over" (v. 14).

The striking and parting of the water is a staged act
here performed without context or comment . . . until we
remember that in the imagination of Israel, the remembered paradigmatic act of parting waters was that of
Moses, who opened the way for emancipation from the
slavery of Pharaoh. In the faithful imagination of Israel,
such a performance as that of Elisha not only brought
back memories of old emancipation but declared in the
present tense that this Elisha now has the capacity to
work for the emancipation and well-being of the peasant
community that had long been exploited by the royal
elites who occupy the rest of the books of Kings. In *Ethics of Liberation: In the Age of Globalization and Exclusion*,
Enrique Dussel notices the way in which remembered
revolutionary practice generates contemporary revolutionary practice. Memory is an empowering generative
force in such social contexts (Dussel 2013, 242–43).

In the paragraph that follows, we may notice two
conclusions drawn by his companions. First, they
observe as a settled conclusion: "The spirit of Elijah
rests on Elisha" (v. 15). Second, they speculate: "it may
be that the spirit of the LORD has caught him up" (v. 16).
Such talk of spirit is explosive and subversive in Israel. It
attests the release of divine power for life, a power that

cannot be contained or domesticated. It is dangerous, but it is also loaded with immense positive potential. It is dangerous because it places in jeopardy all settled power arrangements. It is loaded with possibility that permits the emergence of new forms of social life that were not thinkable or imaginable under the old regime. Thus we are put on notice that what will follow in these narratives is a welling up of transformative power that creates social possibility that could not be generated by the crown, but that also could not be prohibited by royal authority. This is nothing less than an alternative history of social possibility. There is high irony in the fact that we are reading "1 and 2 Kings," but right in the middle of that chronicle is a pause to present the telling of an alternative history that wells up and is welcomed among needy folk. The large attestation of this collection of narratives is that history-making authority is not to be equated with official agents of power. It is more likely the wind (spirit) that blows where it will. It cannot be summoned or curbed. And these narratives bear witness that the spirit (the spirit of Elijah, the spirit of YHWH) sets down upon this uncredentialed character.

Before considering the data, we may pause to reflect on the kind of history this is. Historians are drawn to a recital of official history, of royal time lines and public shows of power. Thus most histories recite kings and nations and empires and wars. (In my experience, even the history of most local church congregations offers a recital of the succession of pastoral leaders . . . or bishops or popes.) But here is an insistence that transformative power is not carried by the credentialed. It is carried rather by the unnoticed who do transformative work that is welcomed and celebrated among its recipients but is often not reckoned by observers as "real." Thus centrist scholarship is inclined to dismiss these prophetic narratives as "legends," which means they are the product of folk imagination (Long 1991, 304, 316). Exactly! But folk imagination can bear witness to a dimension of social reality that will not be carried by or approved by those who occupy the seats of power. In current parlance, such transformation happens through the work of the local community that may not be noticed or respected, and not the work of the government, the corporate economy, or the bureaucracy. These narrative portrayals have a very long life, so that successive generations entertain them in order to have their imagination freed by them in ways that provide a sharp edge over against official power.

What follows in the Elisha narratives after this initial attestation and acknowledgment of his uncommon power is a series of performances that lie outside officialdom. At the outset in 2:19–22 he "heals" bad water, thus assuring a regular supply of water for "the city." The preceding verses suggest that the city is Jericho, but nothing in these verses is that specific.

In chapter 4 we have four narratives of quite local acts of transformation, two of which replicate narratives of Elijah. In 4:1–7, like Elijah, Elisha transforms the life and status of a helpless widow. Only here the narrative situates the crisis in a much more specifically economic way. The crisis now is not that the widow is out of food. It is rather that her creditors are about to seize her son for enslavement as a result of her default on her loan. Elisha reverses her condition by a wonder of olive oil so that she can sell surplus olive oil and thus pay her debt and save her son. Remarkably this telling of the tale has the neighborhood in purview: "Go outside, borrow vessels from all your neighbors, empty vessels and not just a few" (v. 3). We get an image of all of the women in the village mobilizing their pots and pans to help contain the inexhaustible abundance evoked by Elisha. It is a neighborly act done in and with the neighborhood.

The outcome is that the miracle has dazzled the widow and brought well-being for her: "Go sell the oil and pay your debts, and you and your children can live on the rest" (v. 7). Elisha knows the debasing power of debt, and so defies the loan-making establishment, thus making ordinary economics impossible.

In a second episode Elisha, like Elijah, restores the life of a dead son. In this case it is the son of a "wealthy woman." We may assume that the woman had access to all the best credentialed medical care for her son, but none of it worked for him. By contrast, Elisha prayed (v. 33) and breathed on the boy (v. 34), and ended in terse truth: "Take your son" (v. 36). The power for life comes not through "channels," but in ways the community witnesses but does not explain.

In a third episode, Elisha transforms a pot of contaminated stew (vv. 38–41). In a fourth act he feeds a multitude of hungry people with some food left over (vv. 42–44). Loaves abound! (As an addendum to these remarkable acts, we notice in 6:1–7 that Elisha rescued an iron axe head lost in the water. The recovery was a quite practical act, for the axe was the "means of production" for the worker. Elisha's act restored his economic capability.)

The sum of these four local acts is the emergence of abundant life amid an economy of scarcity:

The widow could now pay her debt and save her son.
The wealthy woman could now have her live son back.
The company of prophets could now eat the stew.
A hundred people could now have food with a surplus remaining.

These narratives assert that the reality of life is other than had been taught. It is other than we experienced under the old regime. It is other than the government or the bankers or the doctors had proposed. It is this "otherwise" that evokes narratives that break the grip of royal recital. In Christian attestation, moreover, it is the same otherwise that is featured in the narratives of Jesus, an otherwise that evoked the lethal response of the authorities who did not want or allow the surge of abundant life beyond their administration (see Brodie 2000).

There follow in this narrative interruption of the royal chronicle three extended narratives. In each of them royal power appears, but it appears only in its futility and dysfunction. The import of these narratives is that the real power to generate life lies outside officialdom.

In chapter 5 the narrative of transformation reaches beyond the confines of Israel to concern a Syrian general, Naaman. He is a high-ranking political general in the service of Israel's perennial enemy. He has leprosy, a disease that will render him helpless and beyond political capacity. He cannot find help in the Syrian medical community. The pivot of the narrative is the witness of a young Israelite girl, a captive of war who was a servant in the general's house. She attests to the general that the prophet Elisha in Samaria can heal his leprosy.

He, being a general, goes through channels. He assumes that if there are healing resources in Israel, they will be administered by the king (who in his insignificance is unnamed). The king in Samaria of course cannot heal and dismisses the general's request for healing as a provocation: "Am I God, to give death or life, that this man sends word to me to cure a man of his leprosy? Just look and see how he is trying to pick a quarrel with me" (5:7). This is the abdication of the helpless king.

Attention now focuses on Elisha, who is unimpressed by the general and his entourage. He gives the general the disappointing prescription of healing in the modest Israelite Jordan River: "Go, wash in the Jordan seven times, and your flesh shall be restored and you shall be clean" (v. 10). The general is insulted by the prescription; he had hoped for something more grand and spectacular. But his advisers persuade him to follow the advice of the prophet; he does so and is healed! "So he went down and immersed himself seven times in the Jordan, according to the word of the man of God; his flesh was restored like the flesh of a young boy, and he was clean" (v. 14).

What follows is an exchange about payment for the healing between the general and the prophet. The general, a man of the world who knows about medical copayments, assumes that healing is a business transaction (an assumption shared by the official "medical community") and wants to pay. The prophet insists that the healing is a gift from God and wants no pay. He even blesses the general. In the midst of his immense gratitude to YHWH, the general avers that he will of necessity return to his own god, Rimmon:

> But may the LORD pardon your servant on one count: when my master goes into the house of Rimmon to worship there, leaning on my arm, and I bow down in the house of Rimmon, when I do bow down in the house of Rimmon, may the LORD pardon your servant on this one count. (v. 18)

The unimpressed prophet ends the conversation: "Go in peace." Thus ends the narrative with the general.

In 6:8–23 the Israelites are engaged yet again in the perpetual war with the Syrians (Aram). The Syrian king, unnamed because he is noticeably inconsequential, is frantic about his war effort and fears a security leak about his military plans and strategy. His advisers know that Elisha is the source of the security leak, because he has extraordinary powers of discernment. The king fails in his attempt to arrest Elisha. But Elisha's energy is focused on the Syrian army, which by his prayer is struck blind and rendered ineffective. As a result, the Syrian army is made powerless, through no accomplishment of the Israelite king.

Once the threat of the Syrian army has been halted by their blindness, the narrative reports the very different responses of the king and the prophet to the captives. The king wants to kill the Syrian enemies and addresses Elisha:

Father, shall I kill them? Shall I kill them? (v. 21)

But instead Elisha takes a positive action that breaks, for a time, the cycle of hostility:

> "Set food and water before them so that they may eat and drink; and let them go to their master." So he prepared for them a great feast; after they ate and drank, he sent them on their way, and they went to their master. And the Arameans no longer came raiding into the land of Israel. (vv. 22–23)

The king would perpetuate hostility; the prophet imagines and performs an act that contradicts the conventional royal practice of escalation, entertaining options beyond royal purview.

In the complex narrative of 6:24–7:20 the presenting problem is a famine. It is the responsibility of the royal government to assure a supply of food, and the king does that normally. Of course, famines in every such crisis always impact the poor and vulnerable first. That is because the problem is usually not a complete lack of food, but that scarcity of food produces very high prices for food that the poor cannot pay (Sen 1981). It is no surprise that the story considers two desperate and desperately poor women. They turn to the king for help, a king who is no help at all: "No! Let the LORD help you. How can I help you? From the threshing floor or from the wine press?" (6:27). Beyond that the king voices his rage that the entire problem is caused by Elisha: "So may God do to me, and more, if the head of Elisha son of Shaphat stays on his shoulders today" (6:31). The king is willing to scapegoat Elisha for his own incompetence in supplying food.

So back to prophetic reality: "But Elisha said, 'Hear the word of the LORD: thus says the LORD, Tomorrow about this time a measure of choice meal shall be sold for a shekel, and two measures of barley for a shekel, at the gate of Samaria'" (7:1). Elisha is certain that the price of food will fall drastically, enough that the two women can purchase food. It is a claim disputed by the royal officer (7:2).

Then, through a complex narrative, the food supply of the Syrian army is captured and made available. With plentiful food, the price of food of course is lowered, and the hungry masses surge to get the food: "So a measure of choice meal was sold for a shekel, and two measures of barley for a shekel, according to the word of the LORD" (7:16).

In the mad desperate scramble for food, the royal captain who had contradicted Elisha is trampled to death (7:20); the narrative had put us on notice of this eventuality when Elisha had said earlier to the royal captain: "You shall see it [inexpensive food] with your own eyes, but you shall not eat from it" (7:2).

It is no wonder that the current "food movement" in our society is below the radar of the corporate structure of the economy. It is to be noted, moreover, that in 7:9 the term *gospel* (good news) is used in the report of the lepers about the abundant food supply. This may suggest that the substance of the biblical gospel is especially attuned to material well-being that is a gift of God. Thus Elisha will provide food that the king cannot. The system cannot! Official channels can deliver neither safety nor happiness. These are gifts that arise in local ways outside the official delivery systems.

In contrast to the royal system, Elisha is a performer of abundance in an arena where the royal power fails consistently and completely:

In chapter 5 Elisha will heal as the king cannot.
In chapter 6 Elisha will break the vicious cycle of hostility that the king cannot.
In chapters 6–7 Elisha will provide food that the king cannot (see W. Brueggemann and Hankins 2014).

His aim is regularly the abundant life, especially for those otherwise denied such a life. Thus we get *healed water*, *abundant oil* for the widow, *new life* for the dead son, *purified stew* for the company of the prophets, *food* for a hundred hungry men, *healing* for the general, *recovered means of production* for a worker, *peace* with an enemy, and *food* for desperate women. It is all of a piece! And it all occurs from outside official channels.

Elisha makes no claim for himself. The narrative is clear that the accomplishments of Elisha constitute a performance of the generous will and purpose of YHWH. The claim of the text is that life revolves not around urban structures of power and wealth, but around the elusive power for life given by YHWH, the Lord of creation, given through nondescript hands of human agents. The elusive power from YHWH may well up anywhere in the community and be enacted by unlikely candidates. The narratives dismiss the official power of the king and encourage alternative forms of transformative social power as it is variously given in the life of the community.

It is odd but altogether predictable that, on the death

of Elisha in 13:14–21, the royal narrative immediately resumes in its own chronicle as though nothing different had happened. The continuation of the royal narrative is a "return to normalcy." But the smooth continuity of the royal chronicle cannot silence the continuing power of the interruptive prophetic narrative. It is attested that even contact with "the bones of Elisha" gives life (13:21). The continuing royal chronicle notwithstanding, some in Israel continued to remember that there was and is another source of life to which attention must be paid.

Chapter 5

AUTHORITY

JB: REMEMBER THE KID WHOSE PARENTS LET HIM DO anything? No rules, no curfew, no accountability. He seemed so cool. His parents seemed cool too, at least in the imagination of my other friends and me—because we rarely saw the parents. We were jealous of his freedom. It took some time to realize what was really going on: no rules extended from no attention and no engagement. And no expectations led, well, nowhere.

"The need for authority," declares Richard Sennett, "is basic" (1980, 15). Families, churches, schools, businesses, sports teams, and most other groups need to know what the boundaries of appropriate behavior are. And they need to know who has ultimate responsibility for upholding the rules. Peter Berger (1967) goes so far as to say there is something essentially masochistic about encountering authority. We feel a kind of pleasure being restrained. The pain of running into a boundary assures us of an ordered world that is at least partly knowable. In contrast to being completely lost or isolated, it provides a comforting sense of security. Whether and how people are drawn to accept the claims of those in charge is the problem of authority.

Public discourse today suggests that authority is something to be circumvented. Whether it is Johnny Paycheck, Pink Floyd, or Public Enemy, the imperative to "Question Authority!" finds countless voices. Bosses, parents, spouses, and teachers are the topics of endless jokes and schemes. But the lived necessities and realities of authority are more complicated.

A key issue here is distinguishing authority from power. There are different forms of authority. Max Weber (1958) thought of it in terms of legitimacy, whether it be on the basis of tradition, charisma, or law. By definition, authority is relational. Leadership, as suggested above, requires followership. This is not the case with power, which can be successfully exerted against an involuntarily subjugated victim. A police state keeps order through active coercion.

Not so with legitimate authority, which requires the acquiescence of those who yield. Unlike power, genuine authority does not require a proverbial loaded gun to motivate compliance. For instance, a teacher with authority can leave her classroom and know that her students will behave properly even when she is not there. No group can hold together that does not establish a certain degree of order and trust by way of credible authority.

In our era, this basic need seems to have been

obscured because of the conflation of authority with power. Sennett blames the French. "One of the deepest marks the French Revolution made on modern thinking was to convince us that we must destroy the legitimacy of rulers in order to change their power" (1980, 41). Maybe authority has never been the same.

Immoral power has been lurking for a long time. The horrors depicted in Zamyatin's *We*, Huxley's *Brave New World*, and Orwell's *1984* represent far more than fictional yarns. Real-life monsters like Hitler, Stalin, and Mao armed with concentrated power demonstrated very real threats.

Such fictional and historical precedents were part of the context through which the failures of institutional elites in the middle of the twentieth century were interpreted. The excesses of authoritarianism in the 1940s and 1950s had destructive implications across society. This of course includes fascism and communism, but also the likes of Joseph McCarthy (see Schrecker 1999). Such abuses contributed in no small way to the countercultural movements of the next decade. Failed leadership during the 1960s made matters worse. From Vietnam, the Bay of Pigs, Kent State, Jackson State, and the Nixon White House, for example, Americans learned to be skeptical of their leaders. Closer to home, we became aware of cheating husbands, abusive priests, and embezzling community leaders, who helped give "success" a bad name.

Once the faith in leaders is completely undermined, the resulting skepticism leads to other problems. It is less dramatic, and not accidentally less visible, and less resonant—but the loss of leadership is also important.

Leaders who are too strong are obviously a problem. But the opposite is true too. The cool kid's parents exert no authority, set no expectations, offer no attention, and give no guidance. How do people behave when they are used to attending meetings where no one is in charge? What goes on in communities where the police have no presence? Or the only presence they have is hostile?

In a recent conversation I had with a friend, we were both lamenting that we had each become chairpersons of our respective academic departments, I in the college where I work and she in a public high school nearby. It occurs to me that this itself represents a shift. What used to be thought of as a promotion of sorts in educational institutions is often regarded as a tedious chore now. I suggested to my friend that personnel processes encompassed some of the hardest work. But she said that since she is at a public school, she only hires, she does not fire. I felt a sort of envy because being part of a process that denies someone tenure in college is awful. But I also felt pity for her because she is part of a work culture that has very little accountability. No one is really in charge. We might ponder what factors have led to this situation with public school teachers. What role have teachers themselves, parents, students, administrators, policy makers, unions, and critics of teachers played in helping to weaken the authority of teachers? It is surely complicated. In any case, the consequences are not pretty.

One of the defining features of modernization is the loss of traditional authority. There was a time when American conservatives were known for lamenting this shift. They wanted to *conserve* the organizational authority of those charged with keeping order and maintaining standards. Such respect was afforded to those who evinced the deepest sense of competence, stewardship, citizenship, and vision—not just executives, generals, and senators, but community and family leaders. Such conservatives were especially protective of moral stewards. One should respect one's parents, teachers, priests, or rabbis. The police are there to help. Doctors too. And so on with other professionals. They know what they are talking about.

It is of course the case that liberals—as in the New Deal coalition—have also supported certain kinds of institutional authorities. This includes government, for sure. FDR oversaw the second most significant expansion of the federal government (if you count Lincoln's victories as the first). But liberal respect for authority is not only about the polity. The most important authority is revered for its moral capital. For example, the heroes of the American civil rights movement include lots of special leaders like A. Philip Randolph, Rosa Parks, and Martin Luther King Jr. They were courageous and creative, and put their bodies at risk for a greater cause. In short, across the political spectrum in American society there are different traditions of valorizing moral authority.

But the historical respect for authority—and the necessary sense of engagement, cooperation, and compliance—that made companies, schools, churches, nonprofits, social movements, and ultimately government viable seems to be thinning. This is partly the argument in Robert Putnam's bestseller, *Bowling Alone* (2000). Social capital in America—and its attendant qualities of community, trust, and participation—have declined significantly in recent decades.

Fewer than half of Americans, Gallup (2015) recently reported, have a sense of confidence about most major institutions. This list of institutions that only a minority of Americans trust is eclectic but includes some venerable organizations. They are listed here in order of highest to lowest trust: organized religion, the medical system, the U.S. Supreme Court, the U.S. presidency, public schools, banks, the criminal justice system, newspapers, organized labor, big business, news on the Internet, television news, and the U.S. Congress. The lack of trust in government is now a robust trend. With the exception of one moment after 9/11, the trust Americans have in government in Washington is as low as it has ever been at any time since Watergate (Pew 2014).

As noted above, this loss of trust in institutional authority today no doubt had some basis in the failures of leaders themselves. Naming the worst offenders is no easy task—because there are so many. The astounding corruption of Wall Street executives receiving (or rather giving themselves?) bonuses during a recession they had a hand in creating has to get a nomination. The horrifying record of sexual molestation among Catholic priests and the inexplicable and ongoing cover-up at the highest ranks of church officialdom make the list. The struggles of American schools to provide basic education to our children and keep up with global competition might be considered. Certainly, public school administrators, teachers, and their unions are considered ineffective by a lot of Americans. The violence perpetrated against citizens has naturally led to a crisis of confidence in police.

Mainstream journalism is also tarnished. Whether it is parroting lies about weapons of mass destruction, ignoring signs of recession, consuming and repackaging their own headlines, paying disproportionate attention to demagogues, blurring credible journalism with partisan dogma, or routinely promoting the sensational and profitable over the complex and important, it is no wonder they are near the bottom of Gallup's list. And then there are American politicians of every stripe who utter so much hypocrisy—about the risks of government-supported health care (which they enjoy), the interests of ordinary citizens (which they exploit to their own benefit), the excesses of legislative pork (which they deliver), the need for bipartisanship (which they undermine), the cost of politicizing important issues (which is their stock and trade), or the importance of truth (need I say more?).

But this loss of trust—and the related deterioration of respect for authority—has two other sources, one often associated with the left and one associated with the right. If the French brought into question the legitimacy of rulers some two centuries ago, Americans helped seal the deal a half century ago. The counter-cultural movements of the 1960s have done a good bit of harm to institutional authority (Huntington 1975; Wolfe 2001; Jenkins 2006). For better and for worse, the credibility of the establishment was greatly weakened. Those in charge and the organizations they represent in the private sector, government, and civil society became suspect. What they stood for—power and prestige—was thereafter problematic. The character, expertise, talent, and status previously associated with such achievement no longer had the same currency. The ideal of success itself was hollowed out.

This shift was for the better in so far as afterward Americans felt less inclined to comply with *immoral* authority. The legacy of speaking up for civil rights, women's rights, and workers' rights is still very much with us. In 2000 a stockbroker with the Stanford Group Company named Leyla Wydler started asking questions about a dubious financial product her firm was selling. This eventually led to an investigation and exposure of what looks to have been a large Ponzi scheme. Ms. Wydler was terminated long before the truth surfaced and paid a high price for blowing the whistle (Press 2012). She is in fact a hero. Why people break ranks like that is a complicated matter (see Zimbardo 2007). However hard it remains, though, speaking truth to power became more common after the 1960s.

The shift of the 1960s was for the worse, though, in in so far as thereafter Americans felt less inclined to obey *moral* authority. Alongside the noble causes championed during the sixties, there was a spreading hunger for self-realization and expression. For some, this morphed into self-absorption and resistance to *any* rules. The idea that anyone in charge is untrustworthy, no matter how wise, competent, ethical, or deserving, gained momentum. In the decade that followed, the expression of dissent was increasingly unalloyed by the authentic moral agendas of the sixties. That consequence is in large measure the product of the left.

If some progressives sought to give the past the middle finger, though, the market was more than happy to help find new ways to express that sentiment. As

Thomas Frank details in *The Conquest of Cool,* rebellious
teenagers were not the only ones liberated in the sixties.
Creative advertisers were able to meld dissent, individualism, and consumerism. Being a rebel increasingly
meant affecting a certain look and therefore buying the
right products. Unlike most institutions that surrendered
social influence during this period, the market gained
ground.

Not that it was the main goal, but drowning out the
voices of genuine dissidents amid the chatter of all those
posers was a bonus for agents of the market. This development might have appealed to some conservatives who
favored market logic and disdained the protesters. But
it also created a problem for conservatives protective of
moral traditions. The market hates any memory, reverence, loyalty, or commitment that is not demonstrably
profitable. Moral authority is fine as long as it does not
conflict with the bottom line. This tension, and therefore the logical fault line among modern conservatives,
would intensify in the years to come. Disagreements
among the Wall Street and evangelical factions of the
Republican coalition are one expression of this divide.

Some of these effects from the sixties can be seen in
corporations today. In its purest form, the market does
not discriminate. The social movements of the sixties did
reduce the socially acceptable level of discrimination as
well. This helps account for why the demographic pro-
file of top executives has changed a bit in recent decades.
CEOs are a more diverse group of people now compared
to fifty years ago. But the racial and ethnic minorities and
women who have joined the power elite, most research
suggests, are more likely to have been changed by the

context than to have fostered the transformation of it. The growing diversity at the top may simply have helped legitimate such institutions without changing the basic structure of power or the culture of greed that extends from it (see Zweigenhaft and Domhoff 2011).

In terms of the problem of authority, the main point here is that there is a vast infrastructure effectively maintaining that any authority other than money is not worth much attention (see Satz 2010; Sandel 2012). On one hand, people with moral authority—those attending to the lives of others who evince conviction, altruism, wisdom, and vision—are usually not very ruthless. Think of the wisest family member, teacher, physician, or cleric you know. On the other hand, corporate firms that ultimately have one single commitment (as Milton Friedman famously extolled: "There is one and only one social responsibility of business—to use its resources and engage in activities designed to increase its profits") have raised psychological manipulation to a fine art. Surreptitious data collection, subliminal advertising, product placement, tiered access to the Internet, commercializing holidays and rites of passage, and preying on the emotionally vulnerable are all part of the state of the art. Market fundamentalism provides the philosophical foundation. Profit is the goal. Advertising is the public tool. Lobbying and bribery are the private tools. The point? Trust no one; get as much as you can (see J. Brueggemann 2012b).

If this account is right, then it would make sense that betrayal, scandal, lack of accountability, and amnesia are most welcome dynamics to agents of the market. The less authority and the less trust, the better. This combination works. If we wonder about the origins of hour-long shows and TV channels fully devoted to info-mercials, or the same thing disguised as political com-mentary, the "gotcha" journalism of the 24/7 news cycle, the proliferation of mind-numbing "entertainment news," the fascination with celebrities, including those who are famous simply for being famous, or the general fetishizing of media attention combined with material gain, it should be evident that the lack of credible moral authority is pivotal. As the great defiler Donald Trump observes "There's something very seductive about being a television star" (O'Brien 2005). The unfiltered claims of those trafficking in highly measurable assets such as money, property (clothes, cars, houses), and attention ("friends," "likes," and "followers") trump the fuzzy human values of relationships, morality, and meaning.

It may be profitable for the few. But it is not sustain-able for the many. The problem of authority disturbs different fault lines on the left and on the right. In any case, our current situation in this regard ought to con-cern everyone.

WB: Ours is a culture of loss:

— loss of military hegemony in the world
— loss of the vitality for a growth economy
— loss of what seemed to be a moral consensus
— loss of a sense of neighborliness that sustained the common good

Our society at its best continues to hope for restoration

on all these fronts, but most elementally it hopes for restoration of a neighborly common good in which differences may be contained in a sustainable mutuality.

The counterpoint to these losses in the Old Testament was the destruction of Jerusalem at the hands of the Babylonians in 587 BCE. That event was the defining crisis that characterized the Old Testament. It included a loss of city, temple, and king. It meant the loss of Judah as a viable political identity. Beyond that it meant a new sense of vulnerability about the fidelity of God, the reliability of divine promises, and the assurance of an unconditional status as God's chosen people.

> The Old Testament is the epos of the Fall of Jerusalem. From the first verse of Genesis to the last of Malachi there rings through it the notice of the Capture, the Sack, and the Destruction of the City by the Babylonian Army in 586 B.C. That terrible event is the key to the book. The circumstances which led up to it, the disaster itself, and the consequences which followed, form the subject of the whole. (J. C. Todd, quoted by Gottwald 1954, 63 n. 1)

As a result, all ordered social relationships were put in jeopardy, a jeopardy that impinged on all segments of society:

> Should women eat their offspring,
>   the children they have borne?
> Should priest and prophet be killed
>   in the sanctuary of the Lord?
> The young and the old are lying
>   on the ground in the streets;
> my young women and my young men

have fallen by the sword;
in the day of your anger you have killed them,
    slaughtering without mercy.
        (Lam. 2:20–21; see 1:19; 4:2–4; 5:11–15)

To be sure, the Old Testament is a book of hope. The great prophetic poets of the sixth-century exile offered powerful oracles of a coming future. Indeed, the final verses of the Hebrew Bible (as distinct from the Christian Old Testament) anticipate a full restoration in the land under imperial aegis (2 Chr. 36:22–23). All of that, however, is in prospect but not yet in hand.

In the narrative, Ezra, the defining scribal authority of the period, can assert in a prayer to YHWH a complaint about failed leaders: "Here we are, slaves to this day—slaves in the land that you gave to our ancestors to enjoy its fruit and its good gifts" (Neh. 9:36). And he can voice hope for new possibility:

But now for a brief moment favor has been shown by the LORD our God, who has left us a remnant, and given us a stake in his holy place, in order that he may brighten our eyes and grant us a little sustenance in our slavery. For we are slaves; yet our God has not forsaken us in our slavery, but has extended to us his steadfast love before the kings of Persia, to give us new life to set up the house of our God, to repair its ruins, and to give us a wall in Judea and Jerusalem. (Ezra 9:8–9)

New life will be given; but not yet!

In the wake of the defining loss of Jerusalem, the great poem of Job was likely written (see Balentine 2006;

Seow 2013; Newsom 2003). The book of Job is about loss . . . and possible restoration. The poet, participating in the long tradition of ancient Near Eastern poetry, has transposed the loss and moral and social confusion of Israel into a broader human probe. But the particular Israelite framing of loss is surely in purview in the poem. The poetry of Job turns on loss:

> One day when his sons and daughters were eating and drinking wine in the eldest brother's house, a messenger came to Job and said, "The *oxen* were plowing and the *donkeys* were feeding beside them, and the Sabeans fell on them and carried them off, and killed the servants with the edge of the sword; I alone have escaped to tell you." While he was still speaking, another came and said, "The fire of God fell from heaven and burned up the *sheep* and the *servants*, and consumed them; I alone have escaped to tell you." While he was still speaking, another came and said, "The Chaldeans formed three columns, made a raid on the *camels* and carried them off, and killed the *servants* with the edge of the sword; I alone have escaped to tell you." While he was still speaking, another came and said, "Your *sons* and *daughters* were eating and drinking in their eldest brother's house, and suddenly a great wind came across the desert, struck the four corners of the house, and it fell on the young people, and they are dead; I alone have escaped to tell you." (Job 1:13–20; italics added)

In rapid succession there is loss of oxen and donkeys, sheep and servants, camels, and, finally, sons and daughters. This is Job's wealth, his source of prosperity and wealth, his means of production, and most pitiably, his heirs and point of honor. The paragraph is an undoing of his life, an undoing that refers to the life of Israel in

587, and in our own contemporary reading, the undoing of "life as we have known it."

The severe loss and undoing experienced by Job is the subject and the generator of the long poem that follows. Job's response to loss is one of deep, shrill grief and a wish for death (3:11–19). He imagines that death, with its restful social equality, would be greatly preferable to his current circumstance.

In the presence of his three comforting friends, however, his grief takes the form of dispute and argument. He and his friends continue to share the assumption that the world is morally coherent. Such suffering he knows could only be the product of guilt. Job is agreed to this premise, except that neither he nor his friends have any notion of what sin Job might have committed to evoke such punishment. It has already been asserted and established that he is "blameless and upright" (1:1, 8; 2:3). His friends say to the contrary, and Job agrees but wants specificity.

In his last extended utterance, Job gives a vigorous self-defense against the charges his friends have made against him, and against the very culpability that he himself senses, given his still unshaken assumption about moral coherence (Job 29–31). These three chapters form a rhetorical unit, providing (1) a review of "months of old" (29:2), that is, "the good old days"(chap. 29); (2) the current unbearable situation of suffering, loss, and humiliation (chap. 30); and finally, (3) a vigorous self-defense against his lived experience of loss (chap. 31). There is something both pathos-filled and yet nearly Promethean about the vigor of his self-defense as a rhetorical defiance of his "facts on the ground." The three chapters belong together as a properly ordered social world that contradicts his present circumstance.

In order to appreciate fully his loss in the present, this triad of chapters begins with a long remembering of how it used to be. In that remembered world, Job can recall his social position at the very acme of pride and influence in which he presided over well-ordered and clearly structured social relationships. These structured relationships were (and are?) of immense importance when social status depends on honor and reputation.

- He enjoyed intimacy with God:
    "when the friendship of God was upon
        my tent;
    when the Almighty was still with me."
                                    (29:4b–5a)

- He was surrounded by his children, a source of
  blessing and an assurance about the future:
    "when my children were around me."
                            (v. 5b; see Ps. 127:3–5)

- He was deeply respected in the public domain by
  old and young:
    "When I went out to the gate of the city,
        when I took my seat in the square,
    the young men saw me and withdrew,
        and the aged rose up and stood;
    the nobles refrained from talking,
        and laid their hands on their mouths;
    the voices of princes were hushed,
        and their tongues stuck to the roof of their
            mouths."
                                    (Job 29:7–10)

He was at the pinnacle of social power so that nobles

deferred to him and princes remained silent in his presence. His opinion counted for everything in public transactions; his verdict resolved the public debates, for all heeded his judgment.

Verse 12 is introduced by the particle *ki,* which we translate with NRSV as "because." If it is rendered in this way, we find in verse 12 and thereafter the foundation of his social authority. Old and young, nobles and princes heeded his good word "because." He has established his authority by his decisive contribution to the common good:

> *because* I delivered the poor who cried,
>   and the orphan who had no helper.
> The blessing of the wretched came upon me,
>   and I caused the widow's heart to sing for joy.
>   (vv. 12–13; italics added)

This is a list of the usual suspects—the poor, orphans, widows, wretched—who are to be protected by the strong in the community. Job has performed "justice and righteousness," the indispensable ingredients for a viable social order. Along with the claims of *widow, orphan,* and *poor,* we get the *needy* and the *disabled:*

> I was eyes to the blind,
>   and feet to the lame.
> I was a father to the needy
>   and I championed the cause of the stranger.
>   (vv. 15–16)

Verse 17 suggests that he was an active advocate who took bold steps to break the destructiveness of exploitation:

I broke the fangs of the unrighteous,
and made them drop their prey from their teeth.

As a result, he anticipated a safe, serene, prosperous life filled with honor:

Then I thought, "I shall die in my nest,
and I shall multiply my days like the phoenix;
my roots spread out to the waters,
with the dew all night on my branches;
my glory was fresh with me,
and my bow ever new in my hand."
(vv. 18–20)

It could be that his action (vv. 12–17) and his expectation (vv. 18–20) are a cynical calculation with a guaranteed reward. But the text does not suggest cynicism. It evidences rather a deep trust in the covenantal traditions wherein generous neighborliness yields well-being (see Koch 1983; Schmid 1968). He had a right to expect that! And he got it (vv. 21–25)! He was respected as a chief, as a king, doing what was required for the well-being of all.

Job has entertained the full range of social relationships in a hierarchally ordered society. Nobles and princes, poor and needy, young and old, blind and lame, widow and orphan! All of them are dependent on his justice and righteousness. He is a man of Torah obedience. He is an active practitioner of wisdom that will sustain. He has made a decisive difference for good; if only the tradition had kept its promises.

The transition from chapter 29 to chapter 30 is as abrupt as the shock of Job's reversal. It is as abrupt as the destruction of Jerusalem. It is as abrupt as "the destruction of the middle class" in our society. The "and [NRSV 'but'] now" of 30:1 effectively negates everything that preceded. Job is dumbfounded to discover, in a flash, that none of the good credit he has merited counts for anything. The contrast between "months of old" (29:2) and present circumstance is signaled by the threefold "and now" in verses 1, 9, and 16. "Now" has become unbearable.

The first "and now" is reflection on the young who mock him in his trouble. They are children of nobodies. Job recalls that the fathers of these young people in a previous time were not at all his social equals (vv. 1–8). He voices contempt for their fathers and so disdain for their sons. Proper social distinctions have all collapsed. With the second "and now" (v. 9), the assault on Job is more vigorous, so vigorous that he judges in verse 11 that even God is allied with those against him (vv. 9–15). Their aggression against him has placed in jeopardy both his honor and his prosperity, the very treasures he had valued in chapter 29.

With the third "and now" in verse 16, his restless rage becomes more acute (vv. 16–23). On the one hand, he reaches his limit by describing the impact of their aggression on his body concerning his "bones" (v. 17), his "inward parts" (v. 27), and his "skin" and "bones" (v. 30). But on the other hand, his vitriolic rhetoric has turned from the young who mock him to the God who has turned against him. The very God before whom he maintained honor and well-being now "seizes, grasps," and disregards:

With violence he seizes my garment;

he grasps me by the collar of my tunic.
He has cast me into the mire,
   and I have become like dust and ashes. . . .
You lift me up on the wind, you make me ride on it,
   and you toss me about in the roar of the storm.
                                    (vv. 18–19, 22)

The final part of this rage against circumstance draws
a conclusion that his fate is now darkness, affliction, and
abandonment (vv. 28–31). He is now excluded from
society, left like a wild jackal or an ostracized ostrich,
uncared for and without resources. The end is mourning
and weeping, a contrast to the "sport" (laughter) with
which the chapter began. The rhetoric slowly traces his
complete undoing. His pathos here is in contrast to the
ending of chapter 29, where he comforted those who
mourn. Now he is the one who must mourn. There is
now no support left for him in the social hierarchy that
he had worked so hard to construct and maintain. He
has indeed experienced the loss of respect, loss of sustaining tradition, loss of social reality. His world has
come to an end. And nobody cares, not even God!
   One wonders, in tracing his pathos, how Job had the
gumption to continue to speak in chapter 31 after such
an ending in chapter 30. Except that the poet who writes
his story will not let him finish yet. In chapter 31 we
have his great recital of innocence; he will not entertain
that his sorry state in chapter 30 is merited (see Fohrer
1974). To the contrary, he merits better than that. He
continues to insist that one's location in a social network
should be based on merit. And so he recites his merit,
reiterating much of his virtuous action from chapter 29.

He is not only innocent in what he has not done; he has been a positive, generative force for good.

This chapter of positive self-declaration begins with a series of questions, the answers to which consist in the claim that he merits "portion" and "heritage" from God (vv. 1–4). What follows is a series of conditional statements ("if . . . then") that are in fact assertions that "I have not." Thus he welcomes a world of symmetrical moral rewards and punishments, and insists that the world must be so. The "then" that goes with each "if" is a covenant curse, and he is ready to receive such curses if warranted, precisely because he knows he does not merit them.

He then offers, in this odd rhetorical pattern, a catalog of the ways of generative righteousness upon which society depends:

no falsehood (v. 5)
no guilt of eye (lust) or of hand (greed) (v. 7)
no sexual seduction (v. 9)
no maltreatment of slaves (v. 13)
no disregard of the poor, widow, or orphan (vv. 16–18)
no refusal of clothing for the naked (v. 19)
no abuse of an orphan (v. 21)
no lust for gold (vv. 24–25)
no idolatrous worship of celestial bodies (vv. 26–27)
no exultation over adversaries (vv. 29–30)
no lack of hospitality for strangers (v. 32)
no secret sins (v. 33)
no abuse of the land (v. 38)

Job still expects the old moral tradition to deliver its promise to him.

For that reason his great self-defense ends in 31:35–37 with an insistence that he get a hearing before God, either to learn the charges against him or to have his acquittal verified by God. He does not ask for grace or for forgiveness. He only asks for full and fair justice, for he is, in the construct of the poet, a genuinely righteous man who is as innocent as he says he is. That is how the poem offers him, and nothing tells against that, nothing in his confession, nothing in the probe of his friends, nothing in the court of God. Nothing against him! But he gets nothing in return. The point of this engagement is to make clear that the old symmetrical tradition on which he relies is null and void. His insistence is futile. There will be no validation from the God of heaven, for God is not any longer doing that sort of thing. His moral innocence will no longer get him a cup of coffee. The old ways are exhausted and they will not return. He cannot have the world according to his particular expectations. As in our own time, material loss is not as acutely felt as is anomie, a sense of fundamental disorder. Established forms of moral authority are found to be unreliable. Job's insistence is that the old divine authority that honors his moral merit should prove reliable and responsive. But it is not!

What then? There is a break in the drama that leads us to pause in silence between the challenge of Job and the response of God. That silence is filled by the bombast of Elihu (chaps. 32–37). Only then does God break the silence. The speech of God beginning in chapter 38 disregards Elihu and responds to Job's final statement in chapter 31. The silence is broken by the speech of God, however, in a way that does not answer Job and that does not accommodate his traditional reasoning. It is broken by the tsunami of God's sheer otherness: God will participate in none of Job's categories. The God who now speaks is the God who has no concern for or investment in the old social hierarchies that are kept in place by close moral calculation. Now whatever life remains for Job will be lived in categories other than the ones he can manage.

The whirlwind speeches of God are an avalanche of questions that rush Job and reduce him to timidity and silence. In the presence of this awesome God beyond explanation, Job's moral agenda turns out to be trivial. Now the sweep of questions concerns the mystery of creation that moves exponentially beyond moral calculation or scientific explanation. The questions from God receive no answers from Job. This is a form of authority cast in modes beyond Job's capacity. Job knows nothing that is in the range of the Creator's massive will and purpose. Job has no agency that is remotely commensurate with the agency of the Creator:

> Do you know when the mountain goats give birth?
>   Do you observe the calving of the deer?
> Can you number the months that they fulfill,
>   and do you know the time when they give birth,
> when they crouch to give birth to their offspring,
>   and are delivered of their young? . . .
> Is the wild ox willing to serve you?
>   Will it spend the night at your crib?
> Can you tie it in the furrow with ropes,
>   or will it harrow the valleys after you?
>   (39:1–3, 9–10)

Every question from God requires an honest no from Job that acknowledges God's fundamental difference from him. God does not participate in an authority structure that Job can manage. The speeches of God culminate with the characterization of Behemoth (40:15–24) and Leviathan (41:1–34). Sam Balentine observes of Behemoth:

> God commends Behemoth to Job as a model for what it means to be a creature worthy of the Creator's pride and praise. The lesson for Job seems to be that those who dare to stand before their maker with exceptional strength, proud prerogatives, and fierce trust come as near to realizing God's primordial design for life in this world as is humanly possible to do. (2006, 686)

Balentine calls attention to likeness God finds between this "super beast" and Job as human agent: "Look at Behemoth, which I made just as I made you" (40:15). Behemoth is the only creature in this zoological survey that God introduces with affirmations, not questions. God does not ask Job to do or say anything. He must simply listen, look, and learn from this creature that God has made "just as I made you." When Job looks at Behemoth, he somehow sees himself (2006, 684; see also Balentine 1998).

Behemoth and Job are made the same way! Both of them are equipped by the Creator with strength, prerogative, and trust. Balentine suggests that the divine witness to Behemoth is an invitation to an *alternative humanity* out beyond Job's moral categories. Humanness is the performance of the *bold creatureliness* intended by the Creator and modeled by Behemoth. This is not, to be sure, Promethean autonomy. It is existence in the orbit of God as creature. But it is no longer life according to controllable moral calculations.

Job's final response to the God of the whirlwind is famously ambiguous and problematic. But surely the conventional reading of silent submissiveness is wrong. Balentine undoubtedly has it right:

> I am more inclined to say that what Job has learned is that humankind may image God not by acquiescing to innocent suffering, but rather by protesting it, contending with the powers that occasion it, and, when necessary, taking the fight directly to God. It is just such power, courage, and resolve that God seems to commend to Job in the figures of Behemoth and Leviathan. (Balentine 2006, 698)

Balentine judges human persons as creaturely agents "as near equals of God":

> They too have been created to be fierce and unbridled opponents of injustice, sometimes *with* God, sometimes *against* God, even if it means they will lose the fight. . . . They may speak words of praise; they may speak words of curse. They may also risk moving beyond these levels of discourse to speak words of resistance and protest. . . . But they must not be silent, for silence is unworthy of those who have stood in the divine presence and have learned that creation has been entrusted to them, because they are a "little lower than God." (2006, 698)

At the outset we have seen that Israel, in its demise, hopes for restoration. Thus the poem of Job ends with a prose reflection, the critical status of which is uncertain. In this prose conclusion Job has "spoken rightly" in his challenge to God. Job is not to submit silently to suffering. And then Job receives back from God "twice as much as he had before" (42:10).

> The LORD blessed the latter days of Job more than his beginning; and he had fourteen thousand sheep, six thousand camels, a thousand yoke of oxen, and a thousand donkeys. (v. 12)

And he gets children, seven sons and three daughters. But they are new sons and daughters. He does not get the old ones back.* The new ones do not overcome the loss that lingers. What is restored is different. And Job is to mark the newness differently. He is to value his restored life well beyond the moral calculus of his tradition.

I suggest that in our reading about Job's loss there is an assumption that there will not be a return to the way it was. In the end, the book of Job does not look back. It looks forward. It looks forward to this emancipated human creature who now, along with the Behemoth, is to be generative of newness with fierce trust.

The psalmist affirms:

> Weeping may linger for the night,
> but joy comes with the morning
> (Ps. 30:5)

Lingering weeping lasted a very long time for those who lost Jerusalem, as it did for Job. Newness was not given soon. In our time, weeping over a lost world will linger for a very long time. The biblical tradition, fully

---

*Fackenheim (1980) reads the loss of Job's children as a harbinger of and figure for the six million Jews who perished in the Shoah.

honest about the loss, dares to assert that joy comes in the morning. Not soon, not quickly, perhaps not at daybreak. But it comes; it comes to the human creatures who receive the newness that comes with energy for new possibilities. This is the way of the tradition in which Job is situated. It includes a close moral calculation. But it breaks beyond close moral calculation alongside the God who seeks partners, "almost equals," fierce for the world of new possibilities.

We may imagine Job breaking beyond his close calculations for a different form of community, the one embodied in the fact that even his new daughters can inherit land, doing so alongside his sons, their brothers. Social relationships in new modes become the harbinger of new creation. Job arrives in the presence of a new mode of authority that is not coercive but is beyond his control, that is not explanatory but unendingly generous. Job cannot outflank this authority cast as awesome mystery. He will not want to, because he receives generous gifts and has ample room for his own creaturely authority in the large confines of the Holy.

Chapter 6

SANCTITY

JB: "I don't want to belong to any club that would have me as a member," Groucho Marx explained when he resigned from the Friars' Club of Beverly Hills. Woody Allen paraphrased these words in *Annie Hall* when describing his relationships with women. All enduring relationships have to maintain some sense of mutual self-worth. *We* have to matter or we will not last. Why should I follow the rules of—or, for that matter, join—an organization I do not respect? Why should I play for a team I think is a loser? Why partner with someone I do not like? Groucho makes ironic fun of himself as he invokes a common principle in marketing, the "price-quality inference" or what is sometimes called the "Chivas Regal effect." A high price may sometimes be persuasive in leading to the perception of high quality.

Group membership has costs for individuals. Whether it is dues, taxes, or emotional support, you have to contribute something. If the benefits of being a member are not perceived as substantive, a person may not feel inclined to pay that cost. The implicit purpose of many social norms is to remind us of who *we* are. This is true during the playing of the "Star-Spangled Banner," Thanksgiving dinner, the lighting of the menorah, and the reading of certain bedtime stories, for example. Cooperative traditions remind us that these relationships matter, I am committed to them, and I am invested in the core values around which they revolve. Protecting this bond is the problem of sanctity. Certain values that define our group have to be respected for our group to hold together.

According to the anthropologist A. R. Radcliffe-Brown, "We may say that partaking in the performance of rites serves to cultivate in the individual sentiments on whose existence the social order itself depends" (1961, 955). The most vital rituals pertain to the most important values in a social group. Indeed, the values give rise to the rituals in the first place. But the rituals help those observing them remember what is important to them.

Likewise, certain taboos communicate the worth of an event, relationship, or social role. There are often material advantages from certain prohibitions. For example, one argument for the common incest taboo is marrying someone other than one's sister opens the way for a new alliance with a brother in-law (see Lévi-Strauss 1969, 485). (Marrying one's sibling, needless to say, does not allow for that opportunity.) Sometimes there are physical health concerns behind taboos, too. Marrying outside your immediate family fosters a better gene pool, for instance.

The same point is evident in everyday kinds of etiquette related to food, waste, illness, and sex. Certain norms contribute to at least the perceived impression that their observance makes us more safe. For the most part, we do not cook in the bathroom, have sex in public places, drive off of roads, or greet friends with a kiss when we have the flu. These material and health-based foundations, Jonathan Haidt (2012) argues, originally gave rise to a lot of social ritual, including those attached to the most extreme values. Over time, this connection has been very consequential. The joining of two powerful families through marriage has altered the history of nations. Personal hygiene was a matter of life and death in premodern cities—and sometimes is today during the outbreak of pandemic diseases. Sexual mores still matter for both physiological and psychological reasons.

More generally, a broad range of social norms are related to keeping the body safe. For all the crazy things Americans indulge in (e.g., high heels, fast cars, 40-ounce sodas), a lot of our material culture is immediately beneficial to our physical well-being. This is true of North Face, Honda, and Home Depot, just to name several well-known brands that traffic in material culture and whose products have added to the quality of life for many twenty-first-century Americans. We enjoy

healthier food, cleaner water, warmer clothes, and better shelter than previous generations ever dreamed of.
At least this is true of the modal American experience.
(Kings of another era no doubt lived better than the
homeless of today.) At the risk of stating the obvious,
the point is that substantial aspects of our culture are
quite practical. Sometimes this is readily apparent—as
with accompanying small children to school, wearing
seat belts, or living in structurally sound buildings. But
sometimes it is not. For instance, funeral homes provide
important services in the way of psychological support,
commerce, and public sanitation (Cahill 1999).

As important as the tangible bases of social ritual
are, there is a broad category of motivations that cannot
be easily shown to be materially or medicinally oriented.
Some practices in this category explicitly work against
a material understanding of the world. This kind of
activity bestows symbolic worth on people and under-
scores certain beliefs. "The invention and practice of ritual . . . ," Ernest Becker suggests, "is first and foremost a
technique for promoting the good life and averting evil"
(1975, 6). In our society, ritual inspires casual norms
that remind us we have to look out for the vulnerable.
It influences how we speak to the elderly, the young,
or the infirm, for instance. And it includes ceremonies
that emphasize the significance of certain relationships,
milestones, and values: showers, baptisms, weddings,
funerals, birthdays, graduations, holidays, and so on.
During these special moments, claims are made along
the following lines: certain things about us really matter; *we* matter; what makes us distinctive matters. This

kind of intentional culture constitutes a basic resistance to apathy in social life.

The words *symbol* and *meaning*, Radcliffe-Brown asserts, can be thought of "as coincident. Whatever has a meaning is a symbol and the meaning of whatever is expressed by the symbol" (1961, 954). Which is to say that cultural norms accentuate the meaning of our lives. They tie each ordinary moment to a broader frame of reference in time and space. Sitting down with one's family for the evening meal or saying good morning to a colleague says something about our notions of important relationships, communication, and decency. The practice of *sacred* ritual attempts to tie each extraordinary moment to the broadest frame of reference possible, something we think of in terms of the cosmic, supernatural, or divine. Hence, an attempt is made during the Eucharist, for example, to reiterate the boundless promise of love and how it is necessarily linked to sacrifice for others.

This is not to say that all norms, whether they are ethically significant mores or insignificant folkways, can be interpreted in straightforward, intelligible categories of the material, medical, or symbolic. While much of cultural life has some aspect derived from these kinds of functions, the form it takes is often arbitrary. So not every word sounds like what it means, not every fashion is reducible to a rational motivation, and so on. In other words, culture has an inherently messy quality.

The central values a group reveres and the material expression of those values are negotiated, contested, and interpreted. Rather than a list, recipe, or code, the metaphor we might look to for a culture is a solar system. It has a hot, dense core of meaningful ideals at its center around which various kinds of matter orbit with differing speeds, distances, and trajectories. This is to say that every person in a society is aware of certain defining values in that setting, which they embrace or resist to differing degrees. For the thing to hold together, though, the core must be compelling enough to draw a critical mass of people around it. Without some solid foundation of common values, society is not possible. Without society—its guidance, inspiration, accountability, and support—individuals are in trouble (see Durkheim 1966; Putnam 2000). In short, sanctity matters. It matters for material, medicinal, and symbolic reasons, what can be thought of as distinct categories of normative motivation.

This brings us to our current moment. Several overlapping sources of profanity threaten all three kinds of normative motivations. One is the impulse toward hedonistic individual expression: "I've gotta be me!" John Calvin might call such sensibility *libertine*. This includes behavior unburdened by any concern for moral order as well as behavior explicitly intended to *defy* moral authority. Most college parties exemplify the former category, drag shows fit in the latter. Libertine expression is sometimes associated with the 1960s and the left in general, which is understandable but too simplistic. From Thomas Jefferson to David Petraeus, the Indianapolis 500 and the Kentucky Derby, we can find countless examples that do not fit the stereotype of lefty indulgence. In any event, a lot of damage to persons and property has obviously resulted from defying norms of moderation.

We would certainly not suggest that all social norms should be protected and that an assault on any of them is problematic. What American now thinks women should not have the right to vote? It was an unfair norm supported by an unjust law for most of our country's history. But it is reasonable to expect that the confrontation of an established norm serves some articulated purpose that at least competes with the function of the norm. In effect, the gay community has a rationale for demonstrative pride parades whereas those college students who sometimes drink until they puke do not.

The libertine compulsion can undermine the medical function of social norms. Students at countless colleges across the country end up in the emergency room every weekend after binge drinking. Irreverent behavior—the "hook-up culture" or recreational drugs, for example—can also do psychological harm, which undermines the symbolic function of social norms.

I hasten to add that individual expression, creativity, and fun have great social value. Sometimes we have to act out, just to know we can, just to reassure ourselves that we are not cultural prisoners of our own minds or communities. However, if enough people act out frequently, we can expect serious problems relative to the functions that mainstream institutions and related cultural norms serve.

So this sort of nonnormative behavior carries risks and at times causes significant injury. However, all of this is rather small potatoes compared to the next category of norm-undermining activity, which is pure market behavior. That is, when we make decisions strictly based on the bottom line, without attention to any other human or natural concerns, sooner or later we destroy that which is sanctified.

A rich example is food. The way food is produced, marketed, and consumed in our society often has destructive implications for material, medicinal, and symbolic assets. Fast food, food courts, and sugary breakfast cereals, for instance, are lethal repeat offenders. They rely on fossil fuels for production and transportation. Working conditions in these industries are often unsafe and exploitative. Teams of ingenious advertisers target children in particular to nag their parents and create brand loyalty. In the interest of a warped kind of efficiency, such products have undermined the family meal in particular and American food culture in general. Moreover, some firms do not really sell edible, nourishing food per se, but rather traffic in the notion of "food," such as "all natural non-dairy cream," or "processed cheese product" (see Nestle 2002; Schor 2004; Kilbourne 1999).

From diabetes, obesity, kidney disease, liver disease, heart disease, stroke risks, and various other illnesses, we have clear-cut evidence that Americans are consuming in unhealthy ways. A century ago, the most lethal illnesses in the United States were not well understood. Today, we know a lot about what makes people ill and why they die. And much of it is related to unhealthy diet. Yet we still knowingly produce, market, sell, and consume unhealthy food (Nestle 2002; Poppendieck 2010).

Some might argue that these products serve a need in society—meeting consumer demand (however misguided or manipulated), providing low-cost calories (albeit largely unhealthy), and creating jobs (though often lousy). But it is also clear that in terms of the sanctity of certain norms—think of those related to family gatherings, sustainable consumption, and healthy bodies—they are doing real harm.

Fossil fuels represent a rather large problem related to market logic. If we prioritize efficiency, productivity, and profit in the short run, then the fact that our way of life depends on the use of oil makes perfect sense. But the minute we take into consideration larger concerns, such as ecological sustainability, how climate change is affected by human behavior, and how human behavior is affected by climate change, then we quickly run into problems. More broadly, if we think about how the production and use of fossil fuels affects human society and the well-being of other species, the wonder of nature, God's creation, then this issue clearly becomes a matter of sanctity. The vast majority of scientists concur on the significance of climate change and that human beings are exacerbating the problem. And quite a few scholars believe that this is one of the defining moral problems of our era (see Intergovernmental Panel on Climate Change 2014).

It is as if our beloved home is burning while family members shrilly debate whether it is really all that hot. As that debate rages on, most family members keep bringing fuel into the house to add to the fire. And some of us who feel the heat and recognize it is a dire threat are ourselves adding fuel. Indeed, this is the case at many colleges and universities that cannot figure out how to forgo the use of fossil fuels in their operations or how to divest from fossil fuels in their investments—but deliver extensive curricular and cocurricular programs documenting the problem (Oles 2015).

Food is a type of fuel and fuel is a type of food. Both are fundamental to our way of life. The defilement of the sacred—in this case, that of our bodies and that of our planet—is out in the open for all to see. But it is so ubiquitous and routine that we hardly notice it.

Market-based desecration is manifest in other, less essential aspects of social life as well, including popular culture. Is there any idea, recipe, or formula someone will not use over and over if it is shown to be profitable? Take "reality TV"—please! It started with singing and dancing. Then came fashion, baking, dating, and business. Later it got rough with football, rodeo, and UFC. Now any professional job or serious hobby—tattoo artists, monster makeup, beauty pageants, or weddings—can be perverted and sold via *the formula*. Hey, people want it! What is wrong with that?

The message is simple. Life is a game. Competition is the basic premise. Significant competence is necessary but not sufficient. Self-promotion is also crucial for ultimate achievement. In the end, the only way to win is to make someone else lose. Others who have won are worthy of reverence—even if they relentlessly promote such absurd fantasies, change the rules arbitrarily, belittle the unworthy, and celebrate their own proficiency in this esoteric activity—as the "judges" often do. In this manner, the process of commodification moves beyond the products of work (e.g., cupcakes), to the process of work (e.g., baking), and on to any activity (e.g., dancing, dating, or dwelling together).

There is a way that commodification can add value to a thing or activity. It subjects the phenomenon to market logic, the laws of supply and demand. Whether it is child care, art, or good listening, linking work often not governed by the market to a price structure facilitates professionalization, regulation, and in many cases greater returns. Competition can bring the best out of people, making them more creative and industrious. And it can help get rid of products and activities that no one wants.

But there are limits. Once something is subject to market logic, the main concern shifts from the need it satisfies to whether someone will buy it. One problem is that this logic can undermine concern for the needs of people and how they will be met (see Kuttner 1999; Satz 2010; Sandel 2012).

In an embarrassing fit of frankness, the CEO of Nestlé, Peter Brabeck-Letmathe, once revealed the expansive possibilities he imagined for commodification:

> Water is of course the most important raw material. It is a question of whether we should privatize the normal water supply for the population. And there are two different opinions on the matter. The one option, which I think is extreme, is represented by the NGOs, who bang on about declaring water a public right. That means that as a human being you should

have a right to water. That's an extreme solution.
The other view says that water is a foodstuff like any
other, and like any other foodstuff it should have a
market value. Personally, I believe it's better to give a
foodstuff a value so that we're all aware that it has its
price, and then that one should take specific measures
for the part of the population that has no access to
this water and there are many different possibilities
there. I'm still of the opinion that the biggest social
responsibility of any CEO is to maintain and ensure
the successful and profitable future of his enterprise.
(Wagenhofer 2005).

The problem of course is that when human rights
get linked to the ability to pay, they become distributed according to class. They are no longer inalienable.
"Need" and "deserve" and "buy" all get conflated. If
you cannot buy it, you do not deserve it. If you do not
deserve it, you really do not need it. If you can buy it,
you do deserve it, and so on. According to this logic,
whatever people buy has value—no matter how they
were convinced to buy it, or what the implications of
its use are. This is partly how McDonald's remains an
empire and why pop music outsells classical or jazz.
And it is why bedazzlers, foot tanning machines, and
Velveeta "cheese product" were created in the first place.

A lot of the emphasis these days is on the high end
of consumer goods. See, for example, Paul Nunes and
Brian Johnson's (2004) book, *Mass Affluence*, for relevant
guidance:

Many companies are already benefiting by providing
the moneyed masses offerings designed for occasions
that these consumers will probably never see, but that
are considered worth preparing for—like coats for

summiting Everest (getting more common every day,
right?!) and stoves for preparing the kind of gourmet
meals that demand six burners (some high power,
others with perfect simmer capabilities). (Nunes and
Johnson 2004, 106)

Creating and cultivating a desire for things people
do not need is hardly the worst problem, though. Paying someone for love, voluntarism, God's blessing,
independent judgment, democracy, or freedom is
a self-contradiction. At best, for anything attached
to a nonquantifiable ethic, commodification entails
trivialization.

At worst, it amounts to corruption (Sandel 2012).
This is where sanctity comes into play. Most norms
related to sacred ideals cannot be quantified. The relentless effort to commodify them constitutes moral corruption. This is how we got the commercialization of
Christmas, Hanukkah, Thanksgiving, and other hallowed days (see J. Brueggemann 2012a, 2012c).

But these are only the most extreme examples of
the attempt to grasp what is most special, most meaningful, in human relationships and sell it (see Danziger
2002). This same process unfolds every day in countless social relationships. They may be rather common in
some sense, but the challenges of childhood somehow
feel distinctive for each individual child—and parent.
The same is true of intimate relationships in general:
they are somehow both common and distinctive, with
complicated highs and lows. Likewise with competitive
sports teams, especially one on the cusp of a big achievement. Indeed, this feeling of going through something

singular is a pattern in any substantive human relationship embedded in some real-world challenge.

The moment the activity becomes more about its performance than the main content of the action in the first place, something is lost. That thing is meaning. Thus ritual—in the inherently meaningful, anthropological sense—becomes "ritual"—in the inherently meaningless colloquial sense.

This is what happens when children learning to dance become the subject of "Dance Moms," or during the standard reality fare in which one or both spouses in a married couple offer commentary to the camera about what is going on in their household. Ironically, the mundane activities of a home inevitably become sensationalized and thereby distanced from reality. The meaning of our ordinary lives becomes trivialized through the effort to embellish them into something extra-meaningful. What is a funny pretense on a sitcom like *Modern Family* becomes a cynical schtick among the Kardashians, Chrisleys, or Duggars that undermines our collective understanding of how real relationships actually work.

The same is true of the live coverage of a prechampionship game pep talk from a big-time college sports coach or a microphone shoved in the face of an athlete who won the big match seconds ago. By trying to commodify the authentic moments of social life—to capture and sell them—what is most special about them (they are singularly meaningful to those directly involved) is diminished.

So we get the performance of anxiety, the fabrication

of intimacy, the packaging of victory, and so on. Not just in children's dance competitions, family life, or sports but in a growing swath of social life depicted in popular culture. The ugly irony is that reality TV is not only not real but has the capacity to make actual life less real, which is to say less meaningful. In effect, by fostering a concern for formulaic appearance over content, this kind of cultural expression advances the idea that life is a performance of competition rather than something more substantive (Jackson 2002). All social life entails a kind of performance in which we read cultural scripts taught to us. What shifts in this market-based theater is that we are performing for reasons and audiences that have no bearing on our actual community.

This critique of popular culture may sound grumpy, or even hysterical—or perhaps like a timeless lament from older generations about how misguided younger ones are. I certainly want to acknowledge the social value of amusement, fun, humor, and diversion. There are good reasons why so many people like *Seinfeld*, the March Madness basketball tournament, or *Game of Thrones*, as I do. But I sincerely believe it is worth raising questions about the motivations and consequences related to the cultural products being sold to us. What is the basis of the system that generates the products? What are the implications of their consumption?

To recap, we have explored two forms of defiling social norms: the libertine compulsion and the commodification of social life. Both have pros and cons. In the first case, stretching the boundaries of "decency" can help undermine unjust conventions or just be fun.

But permissive behavior can also be harmful to people and property. In the second case, "fictitious commodification," as Karl Polanyi (1957) calls it, may create jobs and profits, and meet consumer demand. It can also deplete scarce natural resources or trivialize human relationships.

Both of these patterns are destructive in terms of the problem of sanctity, but the commodification of social life is more consequential because it is embedded in a vast infrastructure built deeply into the ground of modern society. Malls, supermarkets, banks, TV, radio, billboards, and the Internet all promote this mind-set. Ultimately, however, the two patterns are largely compatible and at times mutually reinforcing. The latter pattern of commodification encourages the former pattern of self-indulgence, at least the amoral version. "You deserve to have fun and this product will make it happen!" College parties are perfectly aligned with consumption, lots of it. The more conscious, politically motivated libertine activism such as drag performance likely involves more tension with commercialism because the moral purpose of such efforts provides direction that resists mindless consumerism.

In general, public discourse related to the problem of sanctity is rather stunted. The rhetorical terrain devoted to morality revolves almost exclusively around sexuality. It is obviously an important topic. But it is not the only issue. More generally, the thick meaning of human culture cannot be easily measured or categorized. So consideration of its current state in the world requires more rapport and nuance than most public discourse (at least in its current state) can accommodate.

WB: IT IS POSSIBLE TO READ THE BIBLE AS A MANI-
festo about food and the issues of production, distribution, and consumption (Knierim 1995).
The Bible begins with the creation narrative of Genesis
1:1–2:4 that features the blessing of plant and animal
growth:

> Then God said, "Let the earth put forth vegetation:
> plants yielding seed, and fruit trees of every kind on
> earth that bear fruit with the seed in it." And it was
> so. The earth brought forth vegetation: plants yielding
> seed of every kind, and trees of every kind bearing
> fruit with the seed. . . .
> So God created the great sea monsters and every
> living creature that moves, of every kind, with which
> the waters swarm, and every winged bird of every
> kind. And God saw that it was good. God blessed
> them, saying, "Be fruitful and multiply and fill the
> waters in the seas, and let birds multiply on the earth."
> (Gen. 1:11–12, 21–22)

Genesis 1 says the universe was built as a cosmic house
in which the earth could exist as a greenhouse for one
purpose: the provision of vegetation as food for humans
and animals (Knierim 1995, 23).

> The Creator of heaven and earth is the generous
> One who provides food for every living creature. Fur-
> ther, the poem has the capacity to counter the prin-
> ciples of our own culture as they are expressed in
> our dominant system of food production. Currently,
> those principles would seem to be the exact opposite
> of the ones upheld by the Priestly tradition (E. Davis
> 2009, 51).

The Bible anticipates a great end-time banquet in
Jerusalem with rich food for "all peoples":

On this mountain the LORD of hosts will
    make for all peoples
  a feast of rich food, a feast of well-aged
    wines,
  of rich food filled with marrow, of
    well-aged wines strained clear.

                              (Isa. 25:6)

This later expectation is surely reflected in the parable of Jesus concerning all those "who will eat bread in the kingdom of God" (Luke 14:15–24). Among the many images for well-being in time to come under God's good rule, a lavish banquet of welcome is among the most poignant.

Between the *initial blessing of abundant food* in the creation narrative and the *culmination of well-being in God's banquet*, Israel processes the difficult issues of production, distribution, and consumption of food in all of their vexatious practicality.

The creation narrative of Genesis 1, along with other creation texts, attests to an abundance of food that is assured by the faithfulness of the Creator. The only adequate mode of expression for this generous abundance is doxology in which the lavish spillover of glad rhetoric matches the lavish spillover of food that is assured. God has ordered creation to provide ample food: "making it bring forth and sprout, giving seed to the sower and bread to the eater" (Isa. 55:10).

Israel cannot "explain" the mysterious, reliable gift of food; but it can celebrate it and acknowledge that food comes as a gift from beyond us, that is, from God. Thus in Psalm 85:12, in a celebration of divine faithfulness, Israel attests:

> The LORD will give what is good,
>   and our land will yield its increase.

Or Psalm 65 in greater detail:

> You visit the earth and water it,
>   you greatly enrich it;
> the river of God is full of water;
>   you provide the people with grain,
>   for you have prepared it.
> You water its furrows abundantly,
>   settling its ridges,
> softening it with showers,
>   and blessing its growth.
> You crown the year with your bounty;
>   your wagon tracks overflow with richness.
> The pastures of the wilderness overflow,
>   the hills gird themselves with joy,
> the meadows clothe themselves with flocks,
>   the valleys deck themselves with grain,
>   they shout and sing together for joy.
>   (vv. 9–13)

In two extended doxologies the food-giving wonder of creation is acknowledged. Psalm 104 in prescientific mode traces the wonder of creation from the heavens, the waters, and "the earth on its foundations" (vv. 2–5), to grass for cattle and "plants for people to use" (v. 14), to the gifts of wine, olive oil, and bread (v. 15). The consequence of these gifts is human well-being:

> wine to gladden the human heart,
> oil to make the face shine,
>   and bread to strengthen the human heart.
>   (v. 15)

And then, in an exclamatory voice, Israel at praise summarizes the truth of food:

> These all look to you
> to give them their food in due season;
> when you give it to them, they gather it up;
> when you open your hand, they are filled with good
> things.
>
> (vv. 27–28)

Food is for all creatures; it is given in "due season," that is, according to agricultural rhythms; it is a gift and all are filled with it. The imagery suggests a creation satiated because the Creator supplies enough for all. The next verses recognize that creaturely life is dependent on the gift of breath that God gives (vv. 29–30). In this articulation of abundance, there is no dispute, no hoarding, and so no exclusionary scarcity. There is enough all around!

Psalm 104 has its echo in the lyric of Psalm 145. After a generic affirmation of divine fidelity (vv. 4–13), the psalm details that divine fidelity with a series of active verbs of which the creator God is the subject. In verses 13–20 the rhetoric is dominated by the term *all*. No one is excluded; all are welcome. In verses 15–16 specific reference to food echoes the lyric of Psalm 104:

> The eyes of all look to you,
> and you give them their food in due season.
> You open your hand,
> satisfying the desire of every living thing.

All creatures rely on God. All receive food at appropriate times, that is, at harvest (see Gen. 8:22). The Creator is a God of open hands. All are satisfied.

Both Psalms 104 and 135 are unmitigated celebration. It is sober to note, however, that both psalms conclude with a severe warning that is most often skipped over in our appreciation of the doxology:

> Let sinners be consumed from the earth,
>   and let the wicked be no more.
> > (Ps. 104:35)

> All the wicked he will destroy.
> > (Ps. 145:20b)

It is as though the singers of these doxologies knew that the divine assurance of abundant food in the processes of creation is a delicate, fragile matter that can be readily disrupted. No direct connection is made between these severe warnings and the preceding celebrations of ample food. But we know that the "wicked" in both psalms are those who mock Torah commandments and who seek to live an irresponsible life of autonomy. It would be an anachronism to imagine that these verses are precisely concerned with an environmental crisis. And yet if "wickedness" is performed as disregard of God's good arrangement of creation as a matter of self-indulgence, then we can see that the warning is a recognition that the assurance of abundant food through the processes of creation can be disrupted and eventually nullified by Torah violation. Thus "wickedness" as Torah violation is not simply a refusal of commandments, but resistance to the Creator's ordering of creation.

The prophetic oracle of Hosea 4:1–3 makes explicit the connection between Torah obedience and maintenance of good creation, only the matter is stated negatively. In verse 2 the oracle enumerates the commandments of the Decalogue that are systematically violated in Israel:

> Swearing, lying, and murder,
>   and stealing and adultery break out;
>   bloodshed follows bloodshed.

In verse 3 the poet describes the created order that is violated so that it can no longer support plant and animal life, that is, no longer sustain a food supply:

> Therefore the land mourns,
>   and all who live in it languish;
> together with the wild animals
>   and the birds of the air,
>   even the fish of the sea are perishing.

The initial phrase "land mourns" is an idiom for drought. The image is of a creation that shrivels and refuses to perform its generative role. Linkage is made between *Torah violation* and the *ruin of creation* as a food producer. The linkage is with the recurring prophetic "therefore" that is, to be sure, prescientific, but altogether mindful that creation requires responsible human restraint and attentiveness in order that creatureliness may flourish. What is made explicit in the prophetic oracle is tersely acknowledged in the two psalmic warnings. Food provision is a gift of the creation; but reception of such abundance requires a human readiness to act responsively as creatures who depend upon a generative Creator. The doxologies are lyrical, but they are not disconnected from reality. Human creatures have a role to play in sustaining abundant food. That role consists in a recognition of penultimate status on the receiving end of God's good gifts.

The Bible's attestation of abundant food has at its center the faithful generosity of the creator God. But it also has in purview the fact that food is on offer to the community, not to private isolated individuals. Food is for "us," but it is also for all the neighbors. Thus our consumption of food, in the biblical horizon, is always in a triangle of the God who gives, the producer-distributor-consumer who enjoys food, and the neighbor with whom the abundance is shared. The God who gives food is a holy God whose inexplicable generosity must be honored. It is this God to whom gratitude must be addressed, most characteristically in the form of glad obedience. Because the holy God extends food to all creatures (human and nonhuman), the neighbor must be honored and respected and assured of food as well. This triangular arrangement is at the heart of all biblical materiality. It protects food from being reduced to a tradable commodity. Thus the production of food, the distribution of food, and the consumption of food all concern a performed act of triangular fidelity that must not be disrupted or trivialized.

The warning of the Psalms and the realism of the prophetic oracle provides an appropriate segue to the misuse of abundantly given food as a tool of social control. In the narrative of Israel, the very first episode in the life of Abraham and Sarah is a food crisis, that is, a famine. In this narrative the Egyptian pharaoh is the master of the food supply (Gen. 12:10–20). He has adequate resources, due to the Nile, to feed hungry people.

It turns out, however, that Pharaoh imagines himself as autonomous and socially unconnected. He does not see himself as dependent upon or grateful to a food-giving God. Nor is he in any way concerned for neighbors in the food process. As a result, food, to Pharaoh (and his system), is no more than a commodity used for social control. When food is reduced to a commodity, the triangle of fidelity on which humanity depends is distorted and contradicted.

Pharaoh's narrative as world food manager quickly unravels. He imagines, says the prophet Ezekiel, that he is the autonomous owner of the Nile and, therefore, the owner of all the food entrusted to him. YHWH corrects Pharoah and his faulty imagination:

> I am against you,
>   Pharaoh king of Egypt,
> the great dragon sprawling
>   in the midst of its channels,
> saying, "My Nile is my own;
>   I made it for myself."
>   (Ezek. 29:3)

In the Genesis narrative it is this same pharaoh—as an actor of autonomous power—who has a nightmare of scarcity even though he possesses ample food (Gen. 41:1–8). When his two nightmares are interpreted as anxiety about scarcity, that is, about a coming famine, he promptly implements policies, abetted by the Hebrew Joseph, to secure a food monopoly. He does so at the expense of peasants who live a subsistence life. By

Genesis 47 we are told that through the work of his food czar, Joseph, Pharaoh confiscated all the land and all the produce of the land, and all the peasants who worked the land (47:13–26). He does so by forcing the peasants to buy food from his food monopoly. Thus he uses food as a weapon against his own peasants. In the first year of famine, we are told, he sells food to the peasants. In the second year, he takes their cattle in exchange for food; and in the desperate third year of famine, he reduces them to slavery. They have no alternative but to submit to slavery in order that they not starve to death. The abundance of food assured by the Creator has been transposed by Pharaoh into a food monopoly. What might have been free food for needy peasants now becomes a commodity whereby Pharaoh leverages power against the peasants.

Nowhere does the text identify Pharaoh as "the wicked" of Psalms 104:35 and 145:20. But clearly Pharoah comes under the rubric of "the wicked" who does not respect YHWH's generative ordering of creation. He has disrupted the fragile food supply by acting out of his anxiety about scarcity even while he has ample food. It is his anxiety that propelled policies that led to endless accumulation that ended in monopoly. Clearly the doxologies about abundant food do not intend such monopolistic actions that violate the gift.

It does not surprise that Pharaoh's narrative continues in the book of Exodus (just two pages beyond Gen. 47) and moves into violence against the peasants who had been reduced to slavery. Indeed, anxiety about scarcity leads to predatory policies against the vulnerable that end with Pharaoh owning everything and the peasant-slaves living at best a marginal existence. More than that, as Terence Fretheim has observed, Pharaoh turns that life-giving Nile River into a death canal for those whom he fears will threaten his monopoly (Fretheim 2005, 112–13). By his monopoly Pharaoh damages both the human community and the environment that produces food.

The subsequent texts, without explicit reference to Pharaoh, characteristically portray extravagant self-indulgence on the part of the powerful using the imagery of a banquet—sumptuous food that is exhibited and consumed, while the powerful shamelessly dine in the presence of a subsistence peasant economy.

King Belshazzar made a great festival for a thousand of his lords, and he was drinking wine in the presence of the thousand.

> Under the influence of the wine, Belshazzar commanded that they bring in the vessels of gold and silver that his father Nebuchadnezzar had taken out of the temple in Jerusalem, so that the king and his lords, his wives, and his concubines might drink from them. So they brought in the vessels of gold and silver that had been taken out of the temple, the house of God in Jerusalem, and the king and his lords, his wives, and his concubines drank from them. They drank the wine and praised the gods of gold and silver, bronze, iron, wood, and stone.
> (Dan. 5:2–4; see Esth. 7:1–2 and the extravagant food of King Solomon in 1 Kgs. 4:22–23)

Within Israel the prophets regularly indict Israel's elite for their extravagance. Perhaps most poignant of all such indictments is that of Ezekiel, in which he accuses Israel by way of reference to Sodom, "your sister," emblem of all wickedness. But the condemnation of Sodom is not, as we might expect, concerned with sexual matters. Rather: "This was the guilt of your sister Sodom: she and her daughters had pride, excess of food, and prosperous ease, but did not aid the poor and needy" (Ezek. 16:49). The triad of "pride, excess of food, and prosperous ease" go predictably with neglect of the "poor and needy." What had been given in creation as abundance for all now has become the monopoly of the few to the neglect of the many who are vulnerable. Food as gift has become food as weapon. Ezekiel's indictment is an echo of the earlier oracle of Amos in which the prophet anticipates exile for Israel (6:7) because of extravagant self-indulgence (vv. 4–6).

The exodus narrative, Israel's paradigmatic memory, concerns emancipation from the regime of violent monopoly under Pharaoh. As the narrative goes, emancipated Israel ends in the wilderness, that is, outside the domain of Pharaoh's monopoly. In that wilderness that seemed to lack a viable life support system, bread and meat are given! They are given beyond the expectation or explanation of Israel and beyond the will of Pharaoh. They are given in a somewhat elusive, fanciful narrative because any clearer explanatory narrative would succumb to the logic of Pharaoh. Thus:

> In the evening quails came up and covered the camp; and in the morning there was a layer of dew around the camp. When the layer of dew lifted, there on the surface of the wilderness was a fine flaky substance, as fine as frost on the ground. When the Israelites saw it, they said to one another, "What is it?" For they did

not know what it was. Moses said to them, "It is the bread that the LORD has given you to eat."

(Exod. 16:13–15)

This is indeed "wonder bread," given without explanation, about which Israel is left to wonder. The narrative attests that the wilderness, beyond Pharaoh's reach, turns out to be a venue where the creative capacity of YHWH is on exhibit. In this seemingly forsaken venue, YHWH, via Moses, has jump-started creation. As a result there is enough bread for everyone.

> The Israelites did so, some gathering more, some less. But when they measured it with an omer, those who gathered much had nothing over, and those who gathered little had no shortage; they gathered as much as each of them needed.
>
> (vv. 17–18)

The Israelites, however, were not permitted by Moses to store up bread, for storing it up would be to play by the scarcity rules of Pharaoh and not by the abundance protocols of the creator (vv. 19–21).

> The strict prohibition on saving food means that no Israelite tent can be a silo; the Israelite camp cannot be a storage city. The Israelites are to remain dependent on and therefore mindful of God as the One who provides food daily. No wonder Moses was angry when some violated the ban (16:20). The ban on hoarding and manna that spoils overnight are symbols that touch us closely, living as we do in a culture of unprecedented hoarding, consumption, and waste.
>
> (E. Davis 2009, 76)

In the verses that follow, Moses makes provision

for the Sabbath, during which no food is to be gathered (vv. 23–26). The provision of Sabbath rest, an acknowledgment of gifted abundance that requires no work, is a sharp contrast to the work regime of Pharaoh that allows no Sabbath for anyone. "Both forms of restraint enjoined here, not hoarding and Sabbath observance, are meant to heal Israel through daily and weekly acts of recognition that YHWH is God, whose 'hand' is steadily manifested for their good" (E. Davis 2009, 78).

In Christian testimony, the manna narrative of Moses in the wilderness is reperformed by Jesus in the feeding of the multitudes. In Mark 6:30–44 he feeds "five thousand men" with a surplus of twelve baskets. In Mark 8:1–10 he feeds a hungry crowd of four thousand people with a surplus of seven baskets of bread. The hungry are fed. There is no scarcity! The narrative does not explain the abundance of Jesus any more than did Israel explain the manna incident, for explanation is the rhetoric of monopoly. The narrative attestation of Israel (and the early church) defies explanation by asserting a reality grounded in the mystery of God as creator. Israel and the church know that life lived in the abundance of creation—rather than in anxiety about scarcity—makes it possible for all to eat. But the "wicked" never move toward such trustful obedience; they are propelled to monopoly that always ends in predatory violence.

In Luke 12 Jesus tells a story of a man who sought monopoly, who built more and more barns to store up more and more food. It is telling that in the exodus narrative the Hebrew slaves are engaged in building more storehouse cities so that Pharaoh can store more of his food monopoly (Exod. 1:11). Jesus' parable concludes with the outcome that the hoarding man has no future but ends in death. Then, by way of commentary on the parable, Jesus summons his disciples away from anxiety about food:

> Therefore I tell you, do not worry about your life, what you will eat, or about your body, what you will wear. For life is more than food, and the body more than clothing.
>
> (Luke 12:22–23)

Jesus asserts that such anxiety is futile and unproductive. He invites his disciples to an alternative to greed, namely an abundance that the creator God supplies. He notices that nonhuman creatures of God, birds and flowers, know and trust in the endless generative abundance of life.

But of course his disciples do not get the message. In a reflection on the feeding miracles (that is, the Eucharist), the disciples do not understand that where Jesus is, there is ample bread as he has just demonstrated.* They do not understand that the rule of the Creator is an assured abundance to be shared by all. Then he delivers to his disciples the zinger about why they do not understand about the abundance:

> They did not understand about the loaves, but their hearts were hardened.
>
> (Mark 6:52)

---

*The narrative of the feeding miracle is an anticipation of the Eucharist, that is, the Christian sacrament of Holy Communion. The term *Eucharist* means "thanks." Thus the sacrament is an acknowledgment of the gift of food by God that sustains life.

The phrase "hearts were hardened" is likely an allusion back to Pharaoh, who is quintessentially the one with a hard heart. That is, the disciples think like Pharaoh! They think scarcity. They think anxiety. They think hoarding. They do not believe that creation can be jump-started in disadvantaged places. They think that the juices of creation will inevitably yield to the technology of Pharaoh.

And so Jesus, according to Matthew in the same reading as in Luke 12, delivers the durable nonnegotiable either-or about food-abundance-anxiety-scarcity:

> No one can serve two masters; for a slave will either hate the one and love the other, or be devoted to the one and despise the other. You cannot serve God and wealth.
>
> (Matt. 6:24)

One choice is God, the creator of abundance. The other choice is "mammon" (that is the term in the Greek), variously rendered as "capital" or "wealth" (as here from the NRSV) but which refers to autonomy or control and no longer relying on the gifts of creation. The compelling power of Mammon is attested by Jacques Ellul: "That Mammon is a spiritual power is also shown by the way we attribute sacred characteristics to our money. The issue here is not that idols have been built to symbolize money, but simply that for modern man money is one of his 'holy things'" (1984, 77).

The either-or of God or Mammon is a choice of trust or anxiety, of abundance or scarcity, of sharing or predatory possessiveness. The tradition is agreed that anxiety produces greed, and greed is an act of idolatry (trusting false sources of life) that ends in violence and death.

Thus the pharaonic story of accumulation and the manna story of abundance together constitute the biblical paradigm for teaching about food, a paradigm that is reperformed in the New Testament as "greed (which is idolatry)" (Col. 3:5) or as the Eucharist, the great festival of gratitude for abundance (Rosner 2007).

The wonder of the biblical narrative is that neither God the creator nor God's people are outflanked by Pharaoh. When the narrative of *anxiety-scarcity-accumulation-monopoly-violence* is broken, and the abundance of creation is evidenced in the wilderness, it becomes possible to share bread with the neighbor. There is enough for all! Thus in late Isaiah, the prophetic poem castigates self-indulgent worship in Israel that goes with "oppression of all your workers" (Isa. 58:3). The poem summons us to an alternative worship that performs neighborly generosity:

> Is not this the fast that I choose:
>   to loose the bonds of injustice,
>   to undo the thongs of the yoke,
> to let the oppressed go free,
>   and to break every yoke?
> Is it not to share your bread with the hungry,
>   and bring the homeless poor into your house;
> when you see the naked, to cover them,
>   and not to hide yourself from your own kin?
>   (Isa. 58:6–7)

True worship—that is, life in sync with the creator God—concerns sharing material abundance with needy neighbors: bread, house, clothing, all of the indispensables, the very indispensables that Jesus declared to be beyond the reach of anxiety (Luke 12:22–23).

In the Bible and in our own social context, recognition of the community-making, community-maintaining function of food is urgent. Food in the triangle of fidelity is a compelling alternative to food as commodity. Food as commodity acknowledges no God and imagines self-sufficiency. God disappears. And the neighbor disappears as we imagine self-indulgence. When food is a commodity, it is emptied of symbolic, metaphorical capacity, and the process of its production, distribution, and consumption is cheapened. The holy triangle of generosity is contradicted by commoditization.

We have many memberships. But membership in the Jesus movement (like the disciples) is a membership with promises and demands of a quite distinct kind. This membership means commitment to God and belonging to God. That relationship of belonging to God is signified by the term *holy*, which means wholly devoted to God, ready for obedience, and fully prepared to trust; thus "trust and obey"! Such a relationship calls for radical decisions of an either-or kind that allow no middle ground. That either-or as promise invites us to abundance, not scarcity. That same either-or as demand invites us to neighborliness, not selfishness. Thus abundance and neighborliness bespeak belonging to God. It is now the great issue in our food crisis in a predatory economy that is wrecking the environment. That either-or is articulated with great specificity by Jesus:

Then the king will say to those at his right hand, "Come, you that are blessed by my Father, inherit the kingdom prepared for you from the foundation of the world; for I was hungry and you gave me food, I was thirsty and you gave me something to drink, I was a stranger and you welcomed me, I was naked and you gave me clothing, I was sick and you took care of me, I was in prison and you visited me." Then the righteous will answer him, "Lord, when was it that we saw you hungry and gave you food, or thirsty and gave you something to drink? And when was it that we saw you a stranger and welcomed you, or naked and gave you clothing? And when was it that we saw you sick or in prison and visited you?"

(Matt. 25:34–39)

When indeed?!

Such a great analysis! WB continue to inspire me.

10/25/17

CONCLUSION

In conclusion, we offer some reflections on how our different disciplinary perspectives bear on the issues at hand. In particular, we comment on the common ground of sociology and biblical interpretation, what our disciplines have to say to one another, and where they necessarily part company. Each theme in this dialogue is guided by a particular question.

What is the orientation of your disciplinary perspective relative to the dominant order of society?

JB: The perspective of sociology is countercultural, at least in our current setting. The word *sociology*, commonly attributed to Auguste Comte for its formulation, is a hybrid from Latin and Greek. In Latin, a *socius* is a companion, partner, ally, or colleague. When joined with the Greek term -*ology*, the combination refers to the study of companions (Arnush 2015).

The idea of a *socius* is inherently plural. There is no such thing as a single companion. For sociologists, there is always a group. Any variable, event, relationship, or story worth looking at involves a group. And not just any group of strangers, adversaries, or competitors, but two or more people who have some kind of shared interest. We might examine what happens between two strangers, rivals, or armies, but eventually our attention is drawn to what is happening within the home team.

While many of our basic terms in sociology have been assimilated into public discourse—such as *norms*, *culture*, *gender*, and *class*—there is still a divide between the defining ontological presuppositions of sociology and core claims in the American ethos. This is especially true of the overly burdened idea of "American excep-tionalism." For example, to mention the importance of class structure invites immediate condemnation for instigating "class warfare"—even though anyone who seriously studies social inequality comprehends the cen-trality of the concept. To recognize the potential impor-tance of class is to acknowledge that the ideology of the American dream has never been as simple as it sounds. "The sociologist will be driven time and again," Peter Berger declares, "by the very logic of his discipline, to debunk the social systems he is studying" (1963, 38).

This transgressive sensibility in sociology overlaps with the premises of the Bible. You are not alone. You do not make decisions in a vacuum. There are larger forces in play than your own inclinations. And what you see right in front of your face may not be as important as you have been led to believe. To concern oneself with the big picture is antithetical to the atomized, ephemeral orientation so prevalent in our contemporary cultural moment.

This is not to say you, as an individual, do not matter. All the most sophisticated sociological arguments acknowledge the importance of agency, biography, or "personal troubles," as C. Wright Mills (1959) noted. Nor is it to suggest that because you are inevitably situated in and dependent on a group, you should somehow yield to an autocratic state. A sense of mutual interests shared with other people is not the same thing as embracing a particular regime or form of government. The gap between fundamental sociological claims—the dynamics of society matter—and the blinkered individualism of the most facile American dream mythology is evident in such accusations. That is, the premise of "every man for himself" is so strong, to acknowledge the basic collectivist imperative in the human experience is to risk being branded a Stalinist.

WB: The Bible, most particularly the Christian Old Testament alongside the Hebrew Bible in its main flow, is relentlessly subversive. Beginning with the exodus narrative, the text and the God featured in the text witness against the established power of Pharaoh. Subsequently that same subversion, via prophetic imagination, operates against status quo royal Jerusalem and against a succession of predatory regimes—Babylonian, Persian, and eventually Hellenistic.

This biblical text proceeds on the radical affirmation and assumption that the God featured in the text is a real character and a lively agent in the ongoing reality of the historical process. The point is assumed, not argued. It is this covenantal partner as companion who works great transformative wonders in history and who enunciates a clear intentionality to which the world and Israel are summoned. That divine intentionality for social justice is pervasive in the wonders and the commandments of the text. There is no doubt that that divine intentionality, in secular form, is at the heart of the origins of sociology that intended from the outset not to be simply analytic but effectively transformative. The covenantal companionship of God with Israel is a defining model for dialogical existence that refuses easy absolutes and that intends, via strenuous interaction, to generate new social possibility and new social responsibility. The human person envisioned in this text is summoned to be a responsible, free, and effective social agent who shapes and performs an alternative social reality. Thus in its "transgressive orientation" the Bible stands before and alongside sociology in its expectation of a more viable social world.

The biblical text of course is permeated with "exceptionalism" in the form of "chosen Israel," and then "chosen church." But the Bible also recognizes that such chosenness can be pernicious when it takes on a posture of hubris that amounts, in biblical parlance, to idolatry. There is ample ground in the text for sharp critique of contemporary forms of exceptionalism that verge on idolatry. Thus the accent in the biblical text on subversion, companionship, and exceptionalism makes the Bible a ready conversation partner with the sociology that John articulates. The Bible, from the exodus narrative forward, is deeply engaged in something like "class warfare" that, in the rhetoric of a liberation hermeneutic, bespeaks "God's preferential option for the poor." We have so many reasons for engagement between our disciplines!

What is the orientation of your disciplinary perspective relative to the status quo of society and its future?

J B: There is a rich strand of sociological thought that is subversive in a deeper sense—and suspicious of any kind of "chosenness." Critical sociology, which is rooted in Marx's work, regards the dominant order of society as problematic, unnecessary, and eventually soluble. This assumption can be found in much of sociological analysis whether it is in feminist scholarship, queer theory, the study of class stratification, the study of race and ethnicity, the study of social movements, political sociology, economic sociology, environmental sociology, or global political economy—and is woven into the chapters of this book. I regard our current cultural moment related to each of the six foundational moral problems described above to be untenable, but subject to change.

At the heart of the critical tradition is a basic presupposition: humanity is ultimately capable of something better; each of us has the capacity to contribute in constructive ways to the greater good. Marx was speaking about something like this when he commented on the special capacities of human "species-being." (The Quakers' "inner light" somehow comes to mind.) This orientation contradicts other approaches in sociology that accept the ugliness in the human experience as inevitable. Most of that work takes rational self-interest as the starting place in social life. We find this premise evident in much of the sociological research drawing from rational choice theory. Rooted in utilitarian philosophy, however, it has found its most ardent expression in the dominant paradigm of the most influential social science, economics.

Whereas neoclassical economists are embedded in the halls of power—executive offices or boards of directors of private firms, the Federal Reserve, the World Bank, the Department of Treasury, of Commerce, of Labor, and various other governmental offices—critical sociologists would never be offered, generally speaking, nor would they accept invitations to join in such rarified institutions. Needless to say, this is partly about substantive expertise. But it is also about values. It is about what kinds of expertise are valued in different settings. This is how countercultural criticism works for critical sociologists. And it is how establishment ideology works for mainstream economists.

Like critical sociology, the Bible is deeply skeptical about the dominant order. Current arrangements are problematic, unnecessary, and in the end soluble. How the world will be healed is unfathomable. There is no recipe or prescription. But to answer the call of the emancipatory God of the Bible is to nevertheless commit to just this sort of radical hopefulness.

WB: Concerning the Bible, we may parse the term *subversion* precisely. This "sub-*version*" of reality stands against the dominant *version* of reality that is characteristically preoccupied with "wealth, might, and wisdom" (see Jer 9:23–24). The Bible tells an alternative narrative that is indeed "sub-" in the sense that it flies under the radar of dominant control. In this subversive sub-version, Israel without embarrassment places YHWH, the generative emancipatory God, at the center of the narrative. This peculiar and elusive character vouches for, performs, and commands emancipatory justice, mercy, compassion, and generosity that resist the dominant narrative of anxious greed.

That sub-version is offered in the Torah tradition concerning Abraham, Moses, and Israel's arrival at the edge of the land of promise. It remains for the prophets of Israel, however, to make clear in wondrous and elusive ways that this sub-version of reality stands vigorously against and alternative to the dominant royal-priestly narrative of the urban elite. That sub-version is rigorously opposed to the status quo that specializes in injustice and exploitation. It is also powerfully buoyant about alternative social possibility. Long before Martin Luther King Jr. uttered his famous mantra, "I have a dream," prophetic utterance presented the emancipatory God as dreaming and promising an alternative future well beyond present social failure. Like King, these ancient poets believed that such emancipatory utterance was itself generative of new social possibility. Thus they boldly asserted, "The days are coming. . . ."

Is there a single or dominant voice in your perspective?

JB: Sociology does not speak with one voice. Our discipline has a large tent. We are unified by a small set of ontological premises: we are a social species; the group matters; it is complicated but can be studied and illuminated in productive ways; sharing the results of such study is worthwhile. Beyond that, the subject matter is so vast, the tools used for studying it are so diverse, our own role as subjective human beings embedded in our subject matter is so complex, and what we are to do with our findings is so disputed, that we do not have consensus about much else.

There are currently fifty-two official sections in the American Sociological Association, with more in formation. Some revolve around methodology (e.g., Methodology; Comparative and Historical Sociology; Ethnomethodology and Conversation Analysis; Mathematical Sociology), some around theory (e.g., Theory; Rationality and Society), some around a politicized agenda (e.g., Race, Class and Gender; Labor and Labor Movements), some around a "neutral" social problem, if there is such a thing (e.g., Alcohol, Drugs, and Tobacco; Mental Health), some around an institution (e.g., Educational Sociology Medical Sociology; Sociology of Religion), some around a group (e.g., Asia and Asian America; Children and Youth), some around the scope of analysis (e.g., Global and Transnational Sociology; Social Psychology).

Needless to say, we do not all get along. And some do not play nice. Certain sociologists hold such divergent views that fully marginalizing those on the other team seems to be a priority. Quite a few rarely encounter one another's work. And some just do not acknowledge that the others even exist. No one could ever accuse us of a narrow, internally hegemonic consensus.

This multiplicity is regarded by some as a weakness. We periodically hear admonitions, especially from inside sociology, that we sociologists need to get on the same page and explicitly define a core with boundaries so everyone inside can play by the same rules and everyone outside can recognize what we stand for. We covet the unity and status of other disciplines. But the desire for such coherence, focus, and legitimacy is at best elusive and at worst delusional. The social world is vast, fluid, and subject to interpretation. Studying it is hard. What we are doing is complicated and warrants humility and cooperation, as well as conviction and commitment. For that reason, it may well be that the assorted ways our discipline is practiced should be regarded as a sign of integrity and strength. It is also possible that remaining outside the halls of power offers a distinct, unencumbered, and informative vantage point.

Like the scriptures of the Bible, the insights of sociology are collectively rich and varied. In both cases, there is no single text that answers all questions or trumps all other texts. The deepest lessons resist reduction into a simple formula but require careful interpretation, examination, and reconsideration.

W B : The Bible is indeed multivoiced. This is similarly reflected in the multiple program sections of the Society of Biblical Literature. Beyond that, the God of the text speaks in many voices. The coercive passion of church orthodoxy has wanted to reduce the text to a seamless package and to silence all the parts that do not conform. But the text itself insists otherwise. Thus the large themes of the "purity tradition" are in deep tension with the "justice tradition." But in much smaller scale, the text is playful and elusive, and will not permit such reductive silence. In that sense the Bible is like our social reality, which is relentlessly multivoiced.

We have been through a long season of reductive hegemony, but we now know that such silenced voices eventually will speak out. In that same sense, moreover, this multivoiced text is, as Freud saw clearly, not unlike the multivoiced self that may manage to repress unwelcome voices, but they do persist. To honor the multivoiced reality of text, society, and self is indeed unnerving. It is, however, essential to health and to honest dialogue.

The long-standing use of the Bible is to find texts that echo our conviction, ideology, or bias. But responsible reading requires serious engagement with texts that speak otherwise, and that call us away from our too ready absolutes.

What does your discipline have to say about the importance of neighbors?

J B: The transgressive and multivocal qualities of both the Bible and sociology tie into a conception that is central in each context: the neighbor. This idea, which is one of the most repeated terms in the Bible, is the raison d'être of sociology. Margaret Thatcher famously declared that "there is no such thing as society. There are individual men and women, and there are families. And no government can do anything except through people, and people must look to themselves first. It's our duty to look after ourselves and then, also to look after our neighbor." She was laboring to make a point about not overly relying on government. But the statement is self-contradictory. The notion of such an individual actor implies a world—the neighborhood. Just as there is no family member without a family, likewise there is no neighbor without a neighborhood, and no self without a society. Furthermore, such comprehension is evident in her own account: this particular notion of a world, the neighborhood, also entails an ethic—neighborliness.

WB: I am glad that John has underscored the accent on "neighbor." I submit that the "neighbor" is indeed the raison d'être of the Bible, as it is for sociology, because the emancipatory God intends to evoke neighborhood, even in the face of neighbor-destroying ideology. Thus the commandment to "love your neighbor as yourself" (Lev. 19:18) is judged by Jesus to be the second great commandment (Mark 12:31). The Ten Commandments, moreover, culminate with a three-fold mention of "neighbor" as the limit on an acquisitive coveting economy (Exod. 20:17). The notion of "neighbor" does not mean, in biblical parlance, those close at hand with whom we may enjoy intimate and congenial interaction. It means, rather, all the public body of folk who belong to the narrative. Thus Torah-based prophetic imagination envisions that the public economy can and must be organized as a neighborly enterprise that assures each of its members enough for a viable social existence. It has in purview especially the vulnerable, regularly listed as widows, orphans, immigrants, and the poor.

How does your discipline think about the stewardship of the neighborhood?

JB: The countercultural aspect of the neighborhood is in some sense premodern or even antimodern.

It is not a sparkling, new suburban development through which affluent families pass as they move from one job to the next. It is not a short-term playground for tourists, commuters, or entrepreneurs. Rather, the neighborhood implies a durable sense of "us" committed to the stewardship of what makes *this* place and *our* identity special. The neighborhood embodies a kind of *Gemeinschaft*, a specific, idiosyncratic community, that is in tension with modern *Gesellschaft*, the general, impersonal society.

All neighborhoods have a multivocal quality. Both collectively and individually, the voices are esoteric, especially in comparison to the predictable, McDonaldized qualities of *Gesellschaft*. Speech is uttered by many voices. That may involve pressures to keep up with the Joneses, argue, gossip, judge, ridicule, or other strains. It is not necessarily easy. Nevertheless, we have to deal with one another. And in a real neighborhood, our responsibility for our own well-being is inextricably linked to the concern for our neighbors. Hence, the ethic of the neighborhood.

By the way, such a setting is in many ways different from a virtual community. Online, we do not deal with the organic realities of birth, life, or death in the same way. Avoiding hard conversations—and what after all is more important in our most treasured, lasting relationships?—is always one click away. Not so in the neighborhood in which being stuck together is both the best and most challenging thing. We belong here.

In the practice of sociology, the investment in this ethic is expressed in the concern for the common good, or what is sometimes called public goods, public interest, civil society, or shared resources. Sociologists recognize that such concern necessarily involves both what goes on inside the neighborhood as well as external circumstances. We see this in the analyses of various institutions like the family, medicine, religion, government, law, criminal justice, education, and the arts. In each case, there is generally an underlying interest in making things better for a larger number of people. Hence, there is a moral agenda in the vast majority of sociological analyses—even though the language of morality is very much out of vogue in the discipline (see J. Brueggemann 2014).

WB: The familiar distinction of *Gesellschaft* and *Gemeinschaft* is adumbrated in the biblical horizon as "empire and covenantal community." Whereas the empire/*Gesellschaft* may seek to reduce social interaction to commodity transactions through high interest rates, unfair taxation of the vulnerable, and endless debt, the covenant community insists on adequate provision and respect for all, including its most vulnerable members. Thus Israel's most ancient commandments concern how neighbors adjudicate economic inconvenience that they may cause one another (Exod. 21:28–22:15). It follows that the strictures of Deuteronomy require provision for the needy in a way that violates the laws of enclosure that the *Gesellschaft* has put in place (Deut. 24:19–22); the prophetic tradition has the needy neighbor in purview:

> Render true judgments, show kindness and mercy to one another; do not oppress the widow, the orphan,

the alien, or the poor; and do not devise evil in your
hearts against one another.

(Zech. 7:9–10)

And eventually Job, in his self-defense, recites the
obligations one has to the neighborhood that he has fully
honored and performed (Job 31). Every part of the text
intends to resist the reduction of society to commodity
transactions and engagement only with those close at
hand with whom we happen to agree. The biblical tradition, moreover, insists that such covenantal engagement
is not a romantic option only for a specialized community, but that policies and structures of the large economy can be organized for the common good. Thus the
core passions of *Gemeinschaft* may indeed impinge upon
the *Gesellschaft*!

How do sociology and biblical interpretations understand the boundaries of neighborhoods?

JB: Another implication of the centrality of neighbors in both the Bible and sociology is the inev-
itability of *this* neighborhood encountering people from
other neighborhoods. To understand a society, we have
to grasp how its members relate to one another. But we
also have to understand how it is connected to other
societies.

Once we recognize that the neighborhood is elementally important in the human experience, we can
see that the organization of the neighborhood, both its
internal arrangements and its external circumstances,
involves questions of power. What are the obligations
of neighborliness? How far do the boundaries of the

neighborhood extend? What is our obligation to strangers? To adversaries?

How resources are distributed was a defining question among the founders of sociology, including Karl Marx and Max Weber. Both were preoccupied with industrialization and the new economic logic, forms of government and modes of cultural expression that accompanied it. Central to that transformation was a changing stratification system. For Marx, it was those who controlled the engines of economic production that would dominate all institutions. Those without property would sell their labor and thereby add to the profits of the wealthy. Weber recognized the growing power of economic capital too, but also understood that expanding bureaucracy would privilege anyone who could navigate complex organizations, especially in government. Today most scholars who study power and inequality draw in some way from the insights of Marx and Weber.

If Marx and Weber were focused on what drew neighbors into struggle over scarce resources, the other founding sociologist of the "Big Three," Émile Durkheim, was more interested in what drew neighbors together. Following Adam Smith, Durkheim hoped the modern division of labor would facilitate the harmonious coordination of many different kinds of interests and activities. It would be a sense of interdependence that ultimately motivated the individuals in complex, modern society to get along with one another.

Few sociologists today identify particularly with Marx, Weber, or Durkheim per se, but are more inclined to borrow concepts and approaches from different theoretical traditions as needed in different applications.

Still, the debates in sociology about what draws people apart or what draws them together remain vigorous and unresolved.

WB: I am grateful for and instructed by the way in which John brings the three great theorists to our task. Old Testament scholarship has come only late to a critical utilization of such sociological theory in reading the texts. The key breakthrough in such usage of the theorists was the work of Norman Gottwald in *The Tribes of Yahweh* (1979, 622–49). Gottwald appealed particularly to a Marxian analysis to show the way in which Yahwism (reference to the existence and agency of Yahweh, the God of emancipation) was a "function" of a socioeconomic revolution that is portrayed in the exodus narrative. There is no doubt, moreover, that the paradigmatic force of the exodus narrative provided grounds for continuing social criticism and social expectation throughout the biblical tradition. Indeed, a good case has been made that the commandments of Deuteronomy intend that social policy and social structure should serve to ensure a continuing practice of the emancipatory vision of the exodus narrative. Thus the revolution authorized by YHWH continues!

That Marxian analysis helps us to see how it is that a centralized economy in Jerusalem could prey upon the vulnerable peasants, and how it is that the prophetic tradition would critique and expose the confiscatory practices of the urban elite in their predatory abuse of the economically vulnerable. Marxian theory helps us to think systemically about the witness of the text and not reduce it, as is the wont of the religiously romantic, to ad hoc incidents of exploitation in a way that refuses to recognize the systemic reality in the ancient text or in our own context.

But John's appeal to Durkheim has set me thinking in a fresh direction about the visionary, critical practice of the community of covenanted neighbors in which the strong are allied with the weak and the wealthy are in solidarity with the poor. The urgent reasoning of the tradition is concerned first of all not with the economy, but with the neighborhood of real people for which the economy is an indispensable tool. The argument for debt cancellation (Deut. 15:1–18) is a vigorous recognition that the economy must be so subordinated to the needs and requirements of the neighborhood, and that the community must take steps to assure that it does not permit the formation, by default, of a permanent underclass. Such a concern with its stunning requirement of debt cancellation obviously is not based solely on economic considerations, but it is grounded, rather, in human relations that lie beneath economic considerations, even if Marx would not easily allow for anything more elemental than the economic.

In terms of relating this neighborhood to other neighborhoods, the Old Testament does not do very well or go very far with this. Indeed, there is a strong sense of xenophobia that leads to "rules of exclusion" (Deut. 23:3–8). One can, however, see at the edge of the textual tradition an acknowledgment that the great emancipatory force of YHWH extends to other peoples as well, so that the elements of human possibility are not monopolized by Israel (Amos 9:7; Isa.

19:24–25). The series of indictments of other peoples for their brutality in Amos 1–2 indicates that the reach of divine expectation and divine sanction was not based only on the commands of Sinai, but on appeals to a broader, deeper passion about human reality that John Barton (1980; 1998; 2003) terms "natural law." There are surely some things that are not to be done—even if the *Gesellschaft* will tolerate them (e.g., torture)! A durable sense of common humanity pushes well beyond the economic analysis of Marx. Israel does not go far in terms of a global political economy. But much is implied and available when we read with imagination. Marx, Weber, and Durkheim are instructive for our reading. But of course none of those great theorists could take into account the Holy Guarantor of neighborly justice that propels Israel's text. We read with them; and then we read beyond them.

Where do sociology and biblical interpretation necessarily diverge?

JB: The arguments I made above regarding moral foundations share elements of Walter's interpretation of the biblical texts, as previously noted. It should be no surprise as the Bible is deeply sociological; it examines the histories of families, tribes, cultures, governments, economies, religions, migration, wars, rituals, and so many other pertinent topics. Moreover, the founders of sociology—including Marx, Weber, and Durkheim—were informed about and influenced by the Bible, as all learned people of their time were. Each of them came from religious families. Marx and Durkheim were descended from families of distinguished rabbis. Weber was raised in an observant Calvinist family. While all three eschewed religious faith in adulthood, they each understood, in different ways, the power of religious organizations as a social force.

There is a substantive interpenetration between the field of sociology and biblical interpretation. Obviously, though, sociology and the Bible also have significant discontinuities. A relatively young social-scientific discipline and this ancient text offer contrasting ways to understand the world. For starters, they address different questions: How should God guide people's lives? How should society be organized? Though such questions could point in different directions, they need not contradict one another.

However, sociological analysis and religiously engaged biblical interpretation have at least one irreconcilable difference. Most who take the Bible seriously embrace a basic commitment to God's authority. Most who practice sociology draw from the Enlightenment's emphasis on human reasoning. This fundamental distinction has a number of implications. How do we know anything? How do we convince others of what we know? On what basis would we change our minds? Such questions are answered very differently depending on one's vantage point here.

For example, there is a sense of time in Walter's essays that is at once urgent and eternal. This prophetic sensibility can be distinguished from the historicized, contingent sense of time preferred in most sociology. At the core of sociological practice is the scientific method, which seeks to generate cumulative knowledge, to apply and refine theories, so that we learn from the past to illuminate the future. In contrast, Walter's interpretation highlights decisive "pauses" (e.g., sunset, Sabbath), which connote disruptive breakages from previous patterns.

A related contrast is that the hopeful quality of critical sociology is not rooted in God's ultimate fidelity but in an optimistic sense of humanity's basic capacity. What we are waiting for is not the second coming, but an honest reckoning of society's problems and an appropriate realignment of institutional arrangements and cultural norms that allows the better side of human instinct to flourish.

Another implication of this distinction is how comprehensive each orientation is. Sociology has a big tent with many voices. And most of us actually dabble in various theoretical traditions and substantive topics. But I believe that most of us spend lots of time thinking in a manner that is not sociological. At any given moment a professional sociologist may be more or less theoretical, empirical, emotional, artistic, or spiritual. She might worry about health, technology, nature, close relationships, or any range of topics without ever being sociological per se. Indeed, responsible sociology, in my opinion, works hard to apprehend what we are *not* able to see through sociological lenses. In a very fundamental way, that includes any single individual person—who is inevitably the product of many nonsociological forces (e.g., genes, hormones, neurology, weather) as well as sociological ones. The *reason*, as in logic, extending from the Enlightenment that so fundamentally informs sociology, demands such clarification.

In contrast, as Walter comments below, the biblical narrative has a quality that is thicker and more generative. It invites us to ruminate on a broader range of experiences, relationships, and questions and to extrapolate more thoroughly toward new possibilities.

WB: It surely is correct that our two disciplines of sociology and biblical interpretation are in deep tension with each other about most elemental matters. As I have indicated, the two disciplines share a vision of a transformed society, so that it can be recognized that sociology, even for its rigorous commitment to "social-scientific method," has a component of social transformation and betterment at its core.

But that shared vision of social transformation and betterment clearly has very different roots and histories in our two disciplines. And John is no doubt right to see the most elemental distinction in an appeal to *Enlightenment rationality* or to the narrative of a *transformative, emancipatory God*. On that count, our disciplines could not be more unalike.

But we should think with some precision about those differences. On the one hand, a "social-scientific perspective" is wont to conclude that biblical interpretation is grounded in a silly assumption of a crass supernaturalism that no "modern" person could countenance. Such a judgment, however, comes with something like a tin ear, because the God-assumption of biblical interpretation is not directed toward a generic "God," for that argument characteristically turns on "miracles" and "afterlife," neither of which is central to biblical interpretation. Rather, biblical interpretation appeals to a God who is embedded in a quite particular narrative, and this God can only be exposited with reference to that narrative that continues in a dynamic, open-ended way. Thus the "God question" is not about "the existence of God" as the so-called new atheists contend, but it is about the adequacy of the narrative that brings with it a set of memories, norms, disciplines, and expectations. The adequacy or inadequacy of that narrative can only be tested when that narrative—with its memories, norms, disciplines, and expectations—is set alongside or over against other paradigmatic narratives. Such an appeal thus presses Enlightenment rationality also to disclose its paradigmatic narrative, its memories, norms, disciplines, and expectations. When we do that, we can see that both perspectives are thick and complex, and do not admit to simplistic or neat adjudication.

Biblical interpretation, moreover, is not an obscurantist or fideistic enterprise. It has as well a long legacy of critical thought that is rooted in the deep rationality of the great German critics of the nineteenth century who refused and resisted every easy appeal to God-talk. Indeed the great German critics of the nineteenth century arose and worked in the same cultural milieu as the founders of sociology, even if the difference between French and German perspectives mattered to some extent.

Within the discipline of biblical study, the interface of "theological interpretation" and "critical analysis" is a tense and tricky issue. Those of us who do theological interpretation of the Bible are not permitted to choose between theological interpretation and critical analysis. The most compelling "settlement" of this issue that I know is offered by Paul Ricoeur (1967) in his proposal that after we have engaged in critical analysis, we then approach the text with a "a second naiveté" that is not as innocent as a "first naiveté" but is more given to theological claims than a mere critical perspective. Thus in my own practice I conclude that one must be bilingual, speaking the language of critical rigor that allows no "pass" for theological claims, but also speaking the cadences of faith that are sobered and disciplined by criticism. Thus theological interpretation of the Bible is a thick and complex enterprise. There is no "straight line" from ancient text to contemporaneity, and dismissal of that complex process because it does not square with modern rationality is excessively simplistic and reductionist. I hope that in these brief essays I have honored the thick complexity that permits the interpretive enterprise to engage usefully with a social-scientific perspective.

Thus it is my judgment that in both of our disciplines of biblical interpretation and sociology we are obligated on the one hand to be aware of and limited in our subjective confessional perspective; and, on the other hand, we are free to interpret according to our own passionate perspectives, hoping that our critical discipline permits our interpretation to be compelling to those who may look askance at our passionate commitments. I am glad that John and I live in disciplines that continue to call us to account, and that we share passion and hope for the future of our society and of our world. Each of us is situated by the protocols of our disciplines, but we both clearly run beyond those protocols in our passionate commitments.

How do the methods in these fields differ?

J B : We also encounter a cadence in Walter's essays that seems, well, biblical. It has the rhythm and authority of public oration. Like the tirade of a gifted raconteur, it has a creative and untamed character. In contrast, the prose of sociological analysis offered here sounds more like the analysts who write about a speech after it has been given. It is domesticated and contained. This relates back to the point about reason. We sociologists are trained to let the evidence drive the argument. It is the key to credibility. When we reach the limits of evidence, the argument must be delimited. We are also held accountable for attaching our claims to particular theoretical traditions—which often provides a kind of cage that facilitates the domestication of our claims, an "iron cage" of disciplinary approval in some sense.

The rhetorical contrast described here is no doubt due to the oral traditions deeply embedded in the language of the Bible and its subsequent interpretation over many generations compared with the dominant mode of academic prose that is the recent offspring of the Enlightenment. One manifestation of this distinction is that biblical poetry is dominated by words that describe parables, metaphors, and analogies, whereas the Enlightenment-influenced prose encompasses a lot of numbers, which summarize patterns in society. The former illuminates God's creation, which is ultimately mysterious. The latter characterizes the social world, much of which is discoverable

WB: It is surely correct to see that our different perspectives evoke very different patterns and styles of rhetoric. Some of that is of course personal inclination and preference. In large measure, however, it is the limit and requirement of our disciplines, partly a limit and requirement of method, but more fully a limit and requirement imposed by our subject matter. Social-scientific method and data proceed in an analytical way that requires analytical rhetoric. Biblical theological interpretation, by contrast, deals with testimony concerning the inscrutable, elusive character of God, who occupies the text but who will not be contained in or domesticated by safe rhetoric. The rhetoric of biblical theological interpretation, faithful to its subject matter, is, as Paul Ricoeur (1967) sees, testimony that engages in "surplus" that spills beyond "reasonableness." That is, the God given in the biblical text is most appropriately characterized in rhetoric that evidences expansive imaginativeness. Because this God eludes all of our explanatory categories, we can only speak faithfully of this God in cadences that are open and beyond any safe limit, as in the parables of Jesus. In the Old Testament that spillover of rhetoric is given voice in doxologies of exuberant praise and in protests and laments of a profound emotive kind that proceed without restraint. From the oral practice of exuberant praise and unrestrained lament both narrative testimony and prophetic oracle engage in spillover language.

It follows that the interpreter can submit this rhetoric to critical analysis, as many turgid commentaries exhibit. Or interpreters can seek to relay the generative energy of the text by replicating rhetoric. The more one works at relaying that rhetoric and its generative energy, the more one moves away from analytic restraint toward deep expansive constructiveness, and to imaginative figure and image that run beyond critical discourse. John is right to term such rhetoric (my rhetoric) as sounding "like public oration"; or put even more pejoratively, it sounds "sermonic."

We can consider the social function of each of these languages. The restrained rhetoric of sociology, when it is disciplined, is, perforce, analysis that looks backward to report on or describe what is and has been. Such rhetoric has no way of leaning "forward" except by the expectation that a present trajectory in the data will reliably continue. That capacity for extrapolation, however, is not and cannot be generative of future new possibilities. By contrast, the generative anticipatory rhetoric of biblical interpretation that seeks to echo the imaginative and anticipatory rhetoric of the biblical text intends to generate new possibilities that are not mere extensions and extrapolations of what was. Thus the "I have a dream" cadences of Martin Luther King are a fine case in point. King had done analytical work and knew very well about past and present social reality. But he intended to conjure by his daring rhetoric a future that could not be derived from the present or the past.

Such an engagement with the rhetoric of the biblical testimony requires imaginative, emancipatory cadences that social science cannot entertain. Such generative, emancipatory rhetoric at its best, in the text and in belated testimony, serves best as a way to articulate the God who is the subject of such speech, for this God, in the testimony of Israel, is indeed generative and emancipatory. It is the remarkable capacity of such speech, when done honestly and boldly and in trustworthy ways, to evoke newness, a newness that the tradition takes as a gift from the God embedded in the narrative. We do not need to choose between these two practices of speech and indeed dare *not* choose between them. It is crucial to be bilingual. If we have only analytic speech, we will end in despair. If we have only imaginative, generative speech, we will end in illusion. For that reason, I am glad that John and I can together engage in bilingual speech. While he is tilted toward the analytic and I toward the generative and emancipatory, in fact both of us engage in both rhetorics.

How do these perspectives understand reality?

JB: Walter's juxtaposition of looking backward versus forward brings to mind Clifford Geertz's characterization of symbols in his essay "Religion as a Cultural System" (1973, 87–125). Symbols, he explains, function as models in two senses. They serve as models *of* reality, which describe the world, how it *is*, and its history, and help us remember what is important. For instance, the American flag reminds people of Plymouth Rock, Normandy, and 9/11. Symbols also constitute models *for* reality, which prescribe how the world *should* be and guide our behavior accordingly. Thanksgiving reminds us to dwell on what is important and be grateful for the gifts we enjoy, for example.

In sociology and biblical interpretation, we can find both models *of* and *for*. It occurs to me, though, as Walter implies, that sociology is more ambitious about description, about reporting. Our theories are models of reality. Biblical interpretation certainly tells us something about the past. But its enduring resonance derives from its relationship to the future. That is, the enigmatic narrative offers a prescriptive invitation to recognize expansive and heretofore unseen possibilities for how we might live.

As Geertz describes the workings of cultural systems, it becomes clear that we need to look backward and forward, we need to honor certain traditions and be open to new things, we need to wrestle with the gap between *is* and *should*—and we need different ways to see, know, and characterize the world.

WB: I have the sense that as "theory" functions as a model of reality in sociology, so narrative functions as a model of reality in biblical tradition. The "historicity" of Old Testament narratives is now treated in critical fashion with great skepticism. I think, however, that asking historical questions of the narratives is surely the wrong approach, so that all the adrenaline aroused about "historicity" is unhelpful. The narratives are, rather, proposed forms of reality. Thus we may doubt the "historicity" of the exodus narrative; but the exodus narrative need not be taken as "historical." It is rather a script that is waiting to be performed; it is always being given new performance, even in our own time as Michael Walzer (1986) has seen clearly. There is no doubt, moreover, that the great storytellers of the sixth century BCE in ancient Israel were effective in formulating a normative narrative of *exile-and-return* that went well beyond "historical" reality. Even without the benefit of Peter Berger, the storytellers of ancient Israel understood quite well the work of "social construction of reality."

The recognition that *theory* (in John's case) and *narrative* (in my case) function as models gives standing ground for critical assessment of contemporary *models of reality* that are eagerly passed off as *reality*. Thus the claim of "the invisible hand" or "the autonomy of the market" is not a given, but a model of reality to which great loyalty is encouraged. Sociology and biblical study (the latter in the wake of the biblical text itself at the same work) are always adjudicating between models of reality. That adjudication, in both ancient scriptural text and in contemporary culture, requires both courage and imagination, and at its best, a heavy dose of honesty.

In both of our disciplines, we require communication that transcends "tribal commitments and local idiosyncrasies" whether the language of Enlightenment rationality or of cosmic covenantalism. According to biblical testimony, however, such transcendent language is characteristically tempted to flee from socioeconomic reality. For good reason such large language is on the lips of the powerful and elite who are tempted to fly above the quotidian reality of suffering. While we require such transcendent language, we must be suspicious of it and be always drawn back to the specific of narrative in its fresh performance. The Old Testament, in its totality, stretches all the way from narratives and oracles of pain and hope to the great temple liturgies of order and stability. The adrenaline of faith, however, is characteristically evoked by the specific, not by the great majestic phrasings of temple liturgy.

Thus it is not accidental that the current sweeping mantras of globalism are on the lips of the powerful. As Enrique Dussel (2013) has seen so well, globalism is not only visionary; it is also exclusionary. It is the detail of song, narrative, and oracle (that Dussel terms "counterdiscourse") that calls away from grand summary to the concreteness of bodily reality. In biblical testimony, the modeling of reality runs (not unlike Jacob's ladder) up and down, back and forth, between the *dailyness of pain* and the large *promises of well-being*. It is a model that both in its acknowledgment of present reality and in its expectation of alternative possibilities exposes the small tackiness of many contemporary models of reality that compete with it for adherence.

•   •   •

Everyone can see that our current sociopolitical, economic culture is on its way to a death in which humanness shrivels. One can do the hard work of alternative possibility. That hard work will entail both analysis of the facts on the ground and buoyant anticipation of an alternative that is not extrapolated from present circumstance. Such work of critical analysis and anticipation will require the best effort of both of our disciplines and many more, all of which may serve the prospect of an abundant life in the common good.

WORKS CITED

Adams, Samuel L. 2014. *Social and Economic Life in Second Temple Judea*. Louisville: Westminster John Knox.

Agnew, Robert. 1992. "Foundation for a General Strain Theory." *Criminology* 30 (1): 47–87.

———. 1995. "Strain Theory and Crime and Delinquency." Pages 113–38 in *The Legacy of Anomie Theory*. Edited by Freda Adler and William S. Laufer. New Brunswick, NJ: Transaction.

———. 2006. *Pressured into Crime: An Overview of General Strain Theory.* New York: Oxford University Press.

Aguinis, Herman, and Ante Glavas. 2012. "What We Know and Don't Know about Corporate Social Responsibility: A Review and Research Agenda." *Journal of Management* 38: 932–68.

Alterman, Eric. 2004. *When Presidents Lie: A History of Official Deception and Its Consequences.* New York: Viking Penguin.

American Society of Civil Engineers. 2013. "Report Card for America's Infrastructure." www.infrastructurereportcard .org/a/#p/home.

Anderson, Sarah. 2015. "Off the Deep End: The Wall Street Bonus Pool and Low-Wage Workers." Institute for Policy Studies, March 8. www.ips-dc.org/off-the-deep-end-wall -street-bonus-pool-low-wage-workers/.

Arnush, Michael. 2015. Personal Correspondence. Skidmore College. Department of Classics.

Balentine, Samuel E. 1998. "'What Are Human Beings, That You Make So Much of Them?' Divine Disclosure from the Whirlwind: 'Look at Behemoth.'" Pages 259–78 in *God in the Fray: A Tribute to Walter Brueggemann*. Edited by Tod Linafelt and Timothy K. Beal. Minneapolis: Fortress.

———. 2006. *Job*. Smyth & Helwys Bible Commentary. Macon, GA: Smyth & Helwys.

Barton, John. 1980. *Amos' Oracles against the Nations*. Cambridge: Cambridge University Press.

———. 1998. *Ethics and the Old Testament*. Harrisburg: Trinity Press International.

———. 2003. *Understanding Old Testament Ethics*. Louisville: Westminster John Knox Press.

Becker, Ernest. 1975. *Escape from Evil*. New York: Free Press.

Bellah, Robert N. 1999. "Freedom, Coercion, Authority." *Academe* 85 (1): 16–21.

Berger, Peter L. 1963. *Invitation to Sociology: A Humanistic Perspective*. Garden City, NY: Doubleday.

———. 1967. *The Sacred Canopy: Elements of a Sociological Theory of Religion*. Garden City, NY: Doubleday.

Berthoud, Gerald. 2010. "Market." Pages 74–94 in *The Development Dictionary: A Guide to Knowledge as Power*. Edited by Wolfgang Sachs. 2nd ed. New York: Zed.

Bobo, Kim. 2009. *Wage Theft in America*. New York: New Press.

Boer, Roland. 2015. *The Sacred Economy of Ancient Israel*. Louisville: Westminster John Knox.

Bogle, John C. 2005. *The Battle for the Soul of Capitalism*. New Haven: Yale University Press.

Brodie, Thomas L. 2000. *The Crucial Bridge: The Elijah-Elisha Narrative as an Interpretive Synthesis of Genesis–Kings and a Literary Model for the Gospels.* Collegeville, MN: Liturgical Press.

Brooks, David. 2016. "How to Fix Politics." *New York Times,* April 12. www.nytimes.com/2016/04/12/opinion/how-to-fix-politics.html.

Brown, Cliff. 2012. "Poverty in the United States: An Overview." Pages 80–87 in *Inequality in the United States: A Reader.* Edited by John Brueggemann. New York: Allyn and Bacon.

Brueggemann, John. 2012a. "Christmas Post-Mortem: Santa's Attack on the American Family." *Tikkun,* January 1. www.tikkun.org/nextgen/christmas-post-mortem-santas-attack-on-the-american-family.

———. 2012b. *Rich, Free and Miserable: The Failure of Success in America.* Lanham, MD: Rowman & Littlefield.

———. 2012c. "Whose War on Christmas? The Corrosive Power of Cheer and Commerce." *Tikkun,* December 1. www.tikkun.org/nextgen/whose-war-on-christmas-the-corrosive-power-of-cheer-and-commerce.

———. 2014. "Morality, Sociological Discourse, and Public Engagement." *Social Currents* 1: 211–19.

Brueggemann, Walter. 2001. *Testimony to Otherwise: The Witness of Elijah and Elisha.* St. Louis: Chalice.

———. 2005. *Solomon: Israel's Ironic Icon of Human Achievement.* Columbia: University of South Carolina Press.

Brueggemann, Walter, and Davis Hankins. 2014. "The Affirmation of Prophetic Power and Deconstruction of Royal Authority in the Elisha Narratives." *Catholic Biblical Quarterly* 76: 58–76.

Bruni, Frank. 2015. "The Sunny Side of Greed." *New York Times,* July 1. www.nytimes.com/2015/07/01/opinion/frank-bruni-the-good-among-the-greed.html.

Buchheit, Paul. 2013. "5 Industries That Are Hurting America." *Salon,* September 30. www.salon.com/2013/09/30/5_industries_that_are_hurting_america_partner/.

———. 2015. "Inside the Billion-Dollar Brain: 3 Attitudes

That Explain Their Selfish Behavior." *Alternet*, May 10 www.alternet.org/inside-billion-dollar-brain-3-attitudes explain-their-selfish-behavior.

Cahill, Spencer E. 1999. "The Boundaries of Professionalization: The Case of North American Funeral Direction." *Symbolic Interaction* 22: 105–19.

Capaldi, Nicholas. 2005. "Corporate Social Responsibility and the Bottom Line." *International Journal of Social Economics* 32: 408–23.

Carr, Nicholas. 2011. *The Shallows: What the Internet Is Doing to Our Brains.* New York: Norton.

Carter, Stephen L. 1998. *Civility: Manners, Morals, and the Etiquette of Democracy.* New York: Basic Books.

Chetty, Raj, Nathaniel Hendren, Patrick Kline, Emmanuel Saez, and Nick Turner. 2014. "Is the United States Still a Land of Opportunity? Recent Trends in Intergenerational Mobility." *American Economic Review* 104 (5): 141–47.

Collins, Chuck, and Felice Yeskel. 2005. *Economic Apartheid in America.* New York: New Press.

Danziger, Pamela N. 2002. *Why People Buy Things They Don't Need.* Ithaca, NY: Paramount Market.

Davis, Alyssa, and Lawrence Mishel. 2014. "CEO Pay Continues to Rise as Typical Workers Are Paid Less." Economic Policy Institute, June 12. www.epi.org/ publication/ceo-pay-continues-to-rise/.

Davis, Ellen F. 2009. *Scripture, Culture, and Agriculture: An Agrarian Reading of the Bible.* Cambridge: Cambridge University Press.

Domhoff, G. William. 2014. *Who Rules America? The Triumph of the Corporate Rich.* 7th ed. New York: McGraw-Hill.

Dorfman, Jeffrey. 2014. "Dispelling Myths about Income Inequality." *Forbes*, May 8. www.forbes.com/sites/ jeffreydorfman/2014/05/08/dispelling-myths-about -income-inequality/#389cd807292b.

Dorgan, Byron L. 2006. *Take This Job and Ship It: How Corporate Greed and Brain-Dead Politics Are Selling Out America.* New York: St. Martin's Press.

Durkheim, Émile. 1966. *Suicide: A Study in Sociology.* Translated by John A. Spaulding and George Simpson.

Edited by George Simpson. Reprint, New York: Free Press.

———. 1997. *The Division of Labor in Society.* Translated by W. D. Halls. Reprint, New York: Free Press.

Dussel, Enrique. 2013. *Ethics of Liberation: In the Age of Globalization and Exclusion.* Durham: Duke University Press.

Edelman Trust Barometer. 2015. http://www.edelman .com/insights/intellectual-property/2015-edelman-trust -barometer/.

Ellis, Joseph. 2005. *His Excellency: George Washington.* New York: Vintage.

Ellul, Jacques. 1984. *Money & Power.* Translated by LaVonne Neff. Downers Grove, IL: InterVarsity Press.

Erikson, Kai T. 1966. *Wayward Puritans: A Study in the Sociology of Deviance.* Boston: Allyn and Bacon.

Fackenheim, Emil L. 1980. "New Hearts and the Old Covenant: On Some Possibilities of a Fraternal Jewish-Christian Reading of the Jewish Bible Today." Pages 191–205 in *The Divine Helmsman: Studies on God's Control of Human Events, Presented to Lou H. Silberman.* Edited by James L. Crenshaw and Samuel Sandmel. New York: Ktav.

Fohrer, Georg. 1974. "The Righteous Man in Job 31." Pages 1–22 in *Essays in Old Testament Ethics.* Edited by James L. Crenshaw and John T. Willis. New York: Ktav.

Fox, Susannah, and Lee Rainie. 2014. "Part 1: How the Internet Has Woven Itself into American Life." Pew Research Center, February 27. www.pewinternet.org/2014/02/27/ part-1-how-the-internet-has-woven-itself-into-american -life.

Frank, Robert L. 2007. *Richistan: A Journey through the American Wealth Boom and the Lives of the New Rich.* New York: Crown.

Frank, Thomas. 1998. *The Conquest of Cool: Business Culture, Counterculture, and the Rise of Hip Consumerism.* Chicago: University of Chicago Press.

Fretheim, Terence E. 2005. *God and World in the Old Testament: A Relational Theology of Creation.* Nashville: Abingdon.

Frum, David. 2000. *How We Got Here: The 70s—The Decade*

That Brought You Modern Life (for Better or Worse). New York: Basic Books.

Fukuyama, Francis, 1996. *Trust: The Social Virtues and the Creation of Prosperity.* New York: Free Press.

Gallup. 2015. "Confidence in Institutions." http://www.gallup.com/poll/1597/confidence-institutions.aspx.

Geertz, Clifford. 1973. *The Interpretation of Cultures: Selected Essays.* New York: Basic Books.

Gitlin, Todd. 2002. *Media Unlimited: How the Torrent of Images and Sounds Overwhelms Our Lives.* New York: Henry Holt.

Gottwald, Norman K. 1954. *Studies in the Book of Lamentations.* Studies in Biblical Theology 1/14. Chicago: Allenson.

———. 1979. *The Tribes of Yahweh: A Sociology of the Religion of Liberated Israel, 1250–1050 B.C.E.* Maryknoll, NY: Orbis.

Gould, Elise, and Hilary Wething. 2012. "U.S. Poverty Rates Higher, Safety Net Weaker than Peer Countries." Economic Policy Institute, July 24. www.epi.org/publication/ib339-us-poverty-higher-safety-net-weaker/.

Hacker, Jacob S., and Paul Pierson. 2010. *Winner-Take-All Politics.* New York: Simon & Schuster.

Haidt, Jonathan. 2006. *The Happiness Hypothesis: Finding Modern Truth in Ancient Wisdom.* New York: Basic Books.

———. 2007. "The New Synthesis in Moral Psychology." *Science* 316: 998–1001.

———. 2012. *The Righteous Mind: Why Good People Are Divided by Politics and Religion.* New York: Pantheon.

Haidt, Jonathan, and Jesse Graham. 2009. "Planet of the Durkheimians: Where Community, Authority, and Sacredness Are Foundations of Morality." Pages 371–401 in *Social and Psychological Bases of Ideology and System Justification.* Edited by John T. Jost, Aaron C. Kay, and Hulda Thorisdottir. New York: Oxford University Press.

Haidt, Jonathan, and Craig Joseph. 2004. "Intuitive Ethics: How Innately Prepared Intuitions Generate Culturally Variable Virtues." *Daedalus* 13 (4): 55–66.

Hardoon, Deborah. 2015. "Wealth: Having It All and Wanting More." Oxfam International, January 19. https://www.oxfam.org/en/research/wealth-having-it-all-and-wanting-more.

Hersh, Seymour M. 2015. "The Killing of Osama bin Laden." *London Review of Books* 37 (10): 3–12. lrb.co.uk/v37/n10/ seymour-m-hersh/the-killing-of-osama-bin-laden.

Huntington, Samuel P. 1975. "The United States." Pages 59–119 in *The Crisis of Democracy.* Edited by Michael Crozier, Samuel P. Huntington, and Joji Watanuki. New York: New York University Press.

IGM Forum. 2013. "Minimum Wage." www.igmchicago.org/ igm-economic-experts-panel/poll-results?SurveyID=SV_ br01Eq5a9E77NMV.

Intergovernmental Panel on Climate Change. 2014. "Climate Change 2014: Impacts, Adaptation, and Vulnerability." www.ipcc.ch/report/ar5/wg2.

Irons, John. 2009. "Economic Scarring: The Long-Term Impacts of the Recession." Economic Policy Institute Briefing Paper. September 30. www.epi.org/publication/ bp243.

Irwin, Neil. 2013. "This Is a Complete List of Wall Street CEOs Prosecuted for Their Role in the Financial Crisis." *Washington Post,* September 12. https://www .washingtonpost.com/news/wonk/wp/2013/09/12/ this-is-a-complete-list-of-wall-street-ceos-prosecuted-for -their-role-in-the-financial-crisis/.

Jackson, David J. 2002. *Entertainment and Politics: The Influence of Pop Culture on Young Adult Political Socialization.* New York: Peter Lang.

Jenkins, Phillip. 2006. *Decade of Nightmares: The End of the Sixties and the Making of Eighties America.* New York: Oxford University Press.

Kalleberg, Arne L. 2009. "Precarious Work, Insecure Workers: Employment Relations in Transition." *American Sociological Review* 74: 1–22.

Kilbourne, Jean. 1999. *Deadly Persuasion: Why Women and Girls Must Fight the Addictive Power of Advertising.* New York: Free Press.

Knierim, Rolf P. 1995. "Food, Land, and Justice." Pages 225–43 of *The Task of Old Testament Theology: Method and Cases.* Grand Rapids: Eerdmans.

Koch, Klaus. 1983. "Is There a Doctrine of Retribution in

the Old Testament?" Pages 57–87 in *Theodicy in the Old Testament*. Edited by James L. Crenshaw. Philadelphia: Fortrooo.

Kuriloff, Aaron, and Darrell Preston. 2012. "In Stadium Building Spree, U.S. Taxpayers Lose $4 Billion." *Bloomberg Businessweek,* September 5. www.bloomberg.com/news/articles/2012-09-05/in-stadium-building-spree-u-s-taxpayers-lose-4-billion.

Kuttner, Robert. 1999. *Everything for Sale: The Virtues and Limits of Markets.* Reprint, Chicago: University of Chicago Press.

Lasch, Christopher. 1995. *The Revolt of the Elites and the Betrayal of Democracy.* New York: Norton.

Levinas, Emmanuel. 1969. *Totality and Infinity: An Essay on Exteriority.* Translated by Alphonso Lingis. Pittsburgh: Duquesne University Press.

Lévi-Strauss, Claude. 1969. *The Elementary Structures of Kinship.* Rev. ed. Translated by James Harle Bell, John Richard von Sturmer, and Rodney Needham. Edited by Rodney Needham. Boston: Beacon.

Lewis, Michael. 2010. *The Big Short: Inside the Doomsday Machine.* New York: Norton.

Lifton, Robert J. 2011. *Witness to an Extreme Century: A Memoir.* New York: Free Press.

Long, Burke O. 1991. *2 Kings.* Forms of the Old Testament Literature. Grand Rapids: Eerdmans.

Luhby, Tami. 2015. "America's Poor Are 'Envy of the World,' Says Richest Congressman." CNNMoney. money.cnn.com/2015/05/07/news/economy/issa-poor/.

Lukes, Steven. 1973. *Émile Durkheim: His Life and Work.* Reprint, London: Penguin.

Lynch, John, et al. 1998. "Income Inequality and Mortality in Metropolitan Areas of the United States." *American Journal of Public Health* 88: 1074–80.

Madden, Mary. 2014. "Few Feel That the Government or Advertisers Can Be Trusted." Pew Research Center, November 12. www.pewinternet.org/2014/11/12/few-feel-that-the-government-or-advertisers-can-be-trusted/.

Madrick, Jeffrey G. 2011. *Age of Greed: The Triumph of Finance and the Decline of America, 1970 to the Present.* New York: Knopf.

Marwick, Alice E. 2013. *Status Update: Celebrity, Publicity, and Branding in the Social Media Age.* New Haven: Yale University Press.

McIntyre, Robert, Matthew Gardner, and Richard Phillips. 2014. "The Sorry State of Corporate Taxes." Citizens for Tax Justice. www.ctj.org/corporatetaxdodgers/.

McLellan, David. 1971. *The Thought of Karl Marx: An Introduction.* London: Macmillan.

McMillan, Robert. 2014. "What Everyone Gets Wrong in the Debate over Net Neutrality." *Wired,* June 23. www.wired.com/2014/06/net_neutrality_missing/.

———. 2015. "Net Neutrality Won Big Today. But We Can't Get Complacent Just Yet." *Wired,* February 4. www.wired.com/2015/02/net-neutrality-won-big-today-cant-get-complacent-just-yet/.

Merica, Dan. 2014. "Hillary Clinton in 2001: We Were 'Dead Broke.'" CNN Politics. www.cnn.com/2014/06/09/politics/clinton-speeches/.

Messner, Steven F., and Rosenfeld, Richard. 1994. *Crime and the American Dream.* Belmont, CA: Wadsworth.

Mettler, Suzanne. 2010. "Reconstituting the Submerged State: The Challenges of Social Policy Reform in the Obama Era." *Perspectives on Politics* 8: 803–24.

———. 2011. "20,000 Leagues under the State." *Washington Monthly,* July/August. washingtonmonthly.com/magazine/julyaug-2011/20000-leagues-under-the-state/.

Mills, C. Wright. 1959. *The Sociological Imagination.* New York: Oxford University Press.

Moriarty, Shannon, Mazher Ali, Brian Miller, Jessica Morneault, Tim Sullivan, and Michael Young. 2012. "Born on Third Base: What the Forbes 400 Really Says about Economic Equality & Opportunity in America." *United for a Fair Economy,* September 17. d3n8a8pro7vhmx.cloudfront.net/ufe/legacy_url/410/BornOnThirdBase_2012.pdf?1448056427.

Mullainathan, Sendhil, and Eldar Shafir. 2013. *Scarcity: Why Having Too Little Means So Much.* New York: Allen Lane.

National Employment Law Project. 2012. "Big Business, Corporate Profits, and the Minimum Wage." Data Brief. http://nelp.3cdn.net/24hefb45b36b626a7a_v2m6iirxb .pdf.

Nestle, Marion. 2002. *Food Politics: How the Food Industry Influences Nutrition and Health*. Los Angeles: University of California Press.

Newport, Frank. 2015. "Americans Continue to Say U.S. Wealth Distribution Is Unfair." Gallup. http://www.gallup .com/poll/182987/americans-continue-say-wealth -distribution-unfair.aspx.

Newsom, Carol. 2003. *The Book of Job: A Contest of Moral Imaginations*. New York: Oxford University Press.

Nixon, Ron. 2014. "House Approves Farm Bill, Ending a 2-Year Impasse." *New York Times*, January 29. www .nytimes.com/2014/01/30/us/politics/house-approves -farm-bill-ending-2-year-impasse.html?_r=0.

Norton, Michael I., and Dan Ariely. 2011. "Building a Better America—One Wealth Quintile at a Time." *Perspectives on Psychological Science* 6: 9–12.

Nunes, Paul, and Brian Johnson. 2004. *Mass Affluence: Seven New Rules of Marketing to Today's Consumer*. Boston: Harvard Business School Press.

O'Brien, Timothy. 2005. *TrumpNation: The Art of Being the Donald*. New York: Open Road Media.

Oishi, Shigehiro, Selin Kesebir, and Ed Diener. 2011. "Income Inequality and Happiness." *Psychological Science* 22: 1095–1100. doi:10.1177/0956797611417217262.

Oishi, Shigehiro, Ulrich Schimmack, and Ed Diener. 2012. "Progressive Taxation and the Subjective Well-Being of Nations." *Psychological Science* 23: 86–92. doi:10.1177/0956797611420882.

Oles, Thomas P. 2015. "Institutions' Misplaced Fear of Fossil-Fuel Divestment." *Chronicle of Higher Education*, April 2. chronicle.com/blogs/conversation/2015/04/02/ institutions-misplaced-fear-of-fossil-fuel-divestment/.

Olmstead, Kenneth. 2014. "As Digital Ad Sales Grow, News Outlets Get a Smaller Share." Pew Research Center, April 25. www.pewresearch.org/fact-tank/2014/04/25/

as-digital-ad-sales-grow-news-outlets-get-a-smaller
-share/.

Owen, David. 2009. "The Pay Problem." *New Yorker*, October 12, 58–63.

Page, Benjamin I., and Lawrence R. Jacobs. 2009. *Class War? What Americans Really Think about Economic Inequality.* Chicago: University of Chicago Press.

Pareene, Alex. 2012. "Mitt Romney, Self-Made Man." *Salon,* September 18. www.salon.com/2012/09/18/mitt_romney_self_made_man/.

Parsons, Talcott. 1951. *The Social System.* Glencoe, IL: Free Press.

Paxton, Pam. 2005. "Trust in Decline?" *Contexts* 4 (1): 40–46.

Pearson, Christine M., and Christine L. Porath. 2005. "On the Nature, Consequences and Remedies of Workplace Incivility: No Time for 'Nice'? Think Again." *Academy of Management Executive* 19 (1): 7–18.

Pew Research Center. 2014. "Public Trust in Government: 1958–2014." www.people-press.org/2014/11/13/public -trust-in-government/.

Piff, Paul K., Daniel M. Stancato, Stéphane Côté, Rodolfo Mendoza-Denton, and Dacher Keltner. 2012. "Higher Social Class Predicts Increased Unethical Behavior." *Proceedings of the National Academy of Sciences* 109: 4086–91.

Piketty, Thomas. 2014. *Capital in the Twenty-First Century.* Translated by Arthur Goldhammer. Cambridge: Belknap.

Plaskin, Glenn. 2016. "Playboy Interview: Donald Trump (1990)." *Playboy*, March 14. www.playboy.com/articles/playboy-interview-donald-trump-1990.

Polanyi, Karl. 1957. *The Great Transformation.* Reprint, Boston: Beacon.

Poppendieck, Janet. 2010. *Free for All: Fixing School Food in America.* Los Angeles: University of California Press.

Posner, Richard A. 2009. *A Failure of Capitalism: The Crisis of '08 and the Descent into Depression.* Cambridge: Harvard University Press.

Press, Eyal. 2012. *Beautiful Souls: Saying No, Breaking Ranks, and Heeding the Voice of Conscience in Dark Times.* New York: Farrar, Straus and Giroux.

Pugh, Allison J. 2009. *Longing and Belonging: Parents, Children, and Consumer Culture.* Los Angeles: University of California Press

Putnam, Robert D. 2000. *Bowling Alone: The Collapse and Revival of American Community.* New York: Simon & Schuster.

Radcliffe-Brown, A. R. 1961. "On Taboo." Pages 951–58 in vol. 2 of *Theories of Society: Foundations of Modern Sociological Theory.* Edited by Talcott Parsons, Edward Shils, Kaspar D. Naegele, and Jesse R. Pitts. 2 vols. New York: Free Press.

Reader's Digest. 2006. "Best Mother-Son Finish." https://web.archive.org/web/20090523122521/http://www.rd.com:80/your-america-inspiring-people-and-stories/cub-scouts-pinewood-derby-race/article36030.html.

Rector, Robert, and Rachel Sheffield. 2011. "Air Conditioning, Cable TV, and an Xbox: What Is Poverty in the United States Today?" Heritage Foundation, July 19. www.heritage.org/research/reports/2011/07/what-is-poverty.

Reeves, Richard V. 2014. "Equality, Opportunity, and the American Dream." *National Journal*, August 20. https://www.nationaljournal.com/congress/2014/08/20/equality-opportunity-american-dream.

Reichheld, Frederick R. 2001. *The Loyalty Effect: The Hidden Force behind Growth, Profits, and Lasting Value.* Reprint, Boston: Harvard Business Press.

Ricoeur, Paul. 1967. *The Symbolism of Evil.* Boston: Beacon Press.

Rosner, Brian S. 2007. *Greed as Idolatry: The Origin and Meaning of a Pauline Metaphor.* Grand Rapids: Eerdmans.

Rucker, Phillip. 2015. "Bill Clinton Defends Foundation and Paid Speeches: 'I Gotta Pay Our Bills.'" *Washington Post*, May 4. https://www.washingtonpost.com/politics/bill-clinton-defends-foundation-and-paid-speeches-I-gotta-pay-our-bills/2015/05/04/d3d98b4a-f280-11e4-84a6-6d7c67c50db0_story.html.

Saez, Emmanuel. 2015. "Striking It Richer: The Evolution of the Top Incomes in the United States." University of California, Berkeley. Working paper. eml.berkeley.edu/~saez/saez-UStopincomes-2013.pdf.

Saez, Emmanuel, and Gabriel Zucman. 2014. "Wealth Inequality in the United States since 1913: Evidence from Capitalized Income Tax Data." National Bureau of Economic Research. Working Paper no. 20625. www.nber.org/papers/w20625.

Sandel, Michael J. 2012. *What Money Can't Buy: The Moral Limits of Markets.* New York: Farrar, Straus and Giroux.

Saramago, José. 2012. *Raised from the Ground.* Translated by Margaret Jull Costa. New York: Mariner.

Satz, Debra. 2010. *Why Some Things Should Not Be for Sale.* New York: Oxford University Press.

Schmid, H. H. 1968. *Gerechtigkeit als Weltordnung: Hintergrund und Geschichte des alttestamentlichen Gerechtigkeitsbegriffes.* Tübingen: Mohr.

Scheiber, Noam, and Dalia Sussman. 2015. "Inequality Troubles Americans across Party Lines, Times/CBS Poll Finds." *New York Times,* June 3. www.nytimes.com/2015/06/04/business/inequality-a-major-issue-for-americans-times-cbs-poll-finds.html.

Schor, Juliet B. 2004. *Born to Buy: The Commercialized Child and the New Consumer Culture.* New York: Scribner.

Schrecker, Ellen. 1999. *Many Are the Crimes: McCarthyism in America.* Princeton: Princeton University Press.

Sen, Amartya. 1981. *Poverty and Famines: An Essay on Entitlement and Deprivation.* Oxford: Clarendon.

Sennett, Richard. 1980. *Authority.* New York: Knopf.

———. 2006. *The Culture of the New Capitalism.* New Haven: Yale University Press.

Seow, C. L. 2013. *Job 1–21: Interpretation and Commentary.* Grand Rapids: Eerdmans.

Shapiro, Fred R. 2006. *The Yale Book of Quotations.* New Haven: Yale University Press.

Sica, Alan. 2015. "Righting Congress by Writing Congress." *Society (Social Science and Public Policy)* 52: 242–45. doi:10.1007/s12115-015-9894-2.

Soubbotina, Tatyana P., with Katherine A. Sheram. 2000. *Beyond Economic Growth: Meeting the Challenges of Global Development.* Washington, DC: World Bank. www.worldbank.org/depweb/beyond/beyond.htm.

Stanley, Jay. 2010. "Network Neutrality 101: Why the Government Must Act to Preserve the Free and Open Internet." American Civil Liberties Union. https://www.aclu.org/files/assets/ACLU_report_-Network_Neutrality_101_October_2010.pdf.

Stiglitz, Joseph E. 2015. *The Great Divide: Unequal Societies and What We Can Do about Them.* New York: Norton.

Sweet, Ken. 2014. "Median CEO Pay Crosses $10 Million in 2013." *Boston Globe*, May 28. https://www.bostonglobe.com/business/2014/05/27/median-ceo-pay-crosses-million/0l0Gn11lQmepCvo2Noz1TM/story.html.

Tocqueville, Alexis de. 1970. *Democracy in America.* Translated by Henry Reeve. 2 vols. Reprint, New York: Schocken.

Tribe, Lawrence, and Joshua Matz. 2014. *Uncertain Justice: The Roberts Court and the Constitution.* New York: Henry Holt.

Truss, Lynne. 2005. *Talk to the Hand: The Utter Bloody Rudeness of the World Today, or, Six Good Reasons to Stay Home and Bolt the Door.* New York: Gotham.

Uchitelle, Louis. 2006. *The Disposable American: Layoffs and Their Consequences.* New York: Knopf.

United States Department of Labor. 2015. "Minimum Wage Mythbusters." www.dol.gov/featured/minimum-wage/mythbuster.

Wagenhofer, Erwin. 2005. *We Feed the World* (documentary). Grosse Kinomente.

Walzer, Michael. 1986. *Exodus and Revolution.* Reprint, New York: Basic Books.

Weber, Max. 1944. "Max Weber on Bureaucratization in 1909." Pages 127–28 in *Max Weber and German Politics.* Edited by J. P. Mayer. London: Faber & Faber.

———. 1958. "The Three Types of Legitimate Rule." *Berkeley Publications in Society and Institutions* 4 (1): 1–11.

Wilkinson, Richard, and Kate Pickett. 2009. *The Spirit Level: Why Greater Equality Makes Societies Stronger.* New York: Bloomsbury.

Winship, Scott. 2015. "Is the 'Decline' in Men's Earnings behind Marriage's Demise?" *Forbes*, March 16. www.forbes.com/sites/scottwinship/2015/03/16/is-the

-decline-in-mens-earnings-at-the-bottom-behind
-marriages-demise/#693fa514cdbb.
Wolfe, Alan. 2001. *Moral Freedom: The Search for Freedom in a World of Choice.* New York: Norton.
Zimbardo, Philip G. 2007. *The Lucifer Effect: Understanding How Good People Turn Evil.* New York: Random House.
Zweigenhaft, Richard L., and G. William Domhoff. 2011. *The New CEOs: Women, African American, Latino, and Asian American Leaders of Fortune 500 Companies.* Lanham, MD: Rowman & Littlefield.